Collins

Student Support
Materials for
AQA A2 Psychology

Unit 3

Topics in Psychology:
Relationships

th Mike Cardwell
or: Mike Cardwell

Published by Collins Education
An imprint of HarperCollins*Publishers*
77–85 Fulham Palace Road
Hammersmith
London
W6 8JB

Browse the complete Collins Education catalogue at www.collinseducation.com

© HarperCollins*Publishers* Limited 2011

10 9 8 7 6 5 4 3 2 1

ISBN 978-0-00-742161-9

Eleanor Hills and Mike Cardwell assert their moral right to be identified
as the authors of this work.

British Library Cataloguing in Publication Data.
A catalogue record for this publication is available from the British Library.

Commissioned by Charlie Evans and Andrew Campbell
Project managed by Shirley Wakley
Editorial: Hugh Hillyard-Parker
Design and typesetting by G Brasnett, Cambridge
Cover Design by Angela English
Production by Simon Moore
Printed and bound by L.E.G.O. S.p.A. Italy
Indexed by Christine Boylan

Acknowledgements
Every effort has been made to contact the holders of copyright material, but if any have been
inadvertently overlooked the publishers will be pleased to make the necessary arrangements
at the first opportunity.

Credits and Permissions
p. 20 (Fig. 3), Rollie, S. S. & Duck, S. W. (2006), 'Divorce and dissolution of romantic relationships:
Stage models and their imitations', Fine, M. & Harvey, J. (Eds.), *Handbook of divorce and dissolution
of romantic relationships*, 223–240, Mahwah, NJ: Erlbaum; p. 26 (Study), Perilloux, C. & Buss,
D.M. (2008), 'Breaking up romantic relationships: Costs experienced and coping strategies
deployed', *Evolutionary Psychology*, 6(1): 164-181; p. 29 (Study), Clark, R. D., III & Hatfield, E. (1989),
'Gender differences in receptivity to sexual offers', *Journal of Psychology and Human Sexuality*,
2, 39–55, Routledge; p. 31 (Study), Dixson, B.J.; Dixson, A.F., Morgan, B. & Anderson, M.J. (2007),
'Human physique and sexual attractiveness: sexual preferences of men and women in Bakossiland,
Cameroon', *Archives of Sexual Behaviour* 36 (3): 369–75, Springer. doi:10.1007/s10508-006-9093-8;
p. 40 (Fig. 4), Hofstede, G. (1980), *Culture's consequences: International differences in
work-related values*, Beverly Hills, CA: Sage Publications.

Illustrations and photographs
Cover and p. 1, © Greg Hargreaves/gettyimages.co.uk; p. 8, © shutterstock.com/Yuri Arcurs; p. 24,
© shutterstock.com/Yuri Arcurs; p. 25, © iStockphoto.com/Eneri LLC.

Contents

The reward/need satisfaction model

This theory was suggested by Byrne and Clore (1970), who stressed the reward and satisfaction of needs we receive when in relationships. Initially, the rewarding aspects of the relationship are emphasized and, in the short term, it is these that help the formation of the relationship. If there is no, or little, reward, then the formation does not occur. This formation is based around the behaviourist principles of **operant** and **classical conditioning**.

Operant conditioning

According to operant conditioning, if a behaviour is followed by a desirable consequence, it becomes more frequent; if it is followed by an undesirable consequence, it becomes less frequent. Being in a relationship is **positively reinforced** as it brings a variety of rewards, such as companionship, sex and intimacy. It is also **negatively reinforced** by the individual not wanting to be lonely or sad.

The rewards we get from relationships are not always as apparent to other people as would be a more tangible reward such as financial security; they may be subtler. For example, if we form a relationship with someone who agrees with our opinions on politics, this serves us two ways:

- It will raise our self-esteem, as we have an ally.
- There is also negative reinforcement, as we know that heated arguments about politics are not likely to occur.

Even if someone is dominant or 'bossy' in the relationship, this may serve both partners well. For the 'bossy' one, it will satisfy their need to dominate; for the one being bossed, they may have a need to let someone else make the decisions.

Classical conditioning

Classical conditioning is a form of learning where a neutral stimulus is paired with a stimulus that already produces a response, such that, over time, the neutral stimulus also produces that response. Figure 1 illustrates how the process of classical conditioning in relationship formation might occur.

In this example, prior to conditioning, Robert (neutral stimulus) would not prompt a response in Natalie as she doesn't know him. Parties always make Natalie feel happy, so they act as the unconditioned stimulus. At a really good party, Natalie meets Robert and starts to associate him with the happy feeling she has at that time. Subsequently, whenever she meets Robert (now the conditioned stimulus), she will feel happy (conditioned response). Natalie is, therefore, more likely to form a relationship with him.

Essential notes

It is the 'reward' aspect of the reward/need satisfaction model that needs to be emphasized when talking about formation of relationships. The 'need' aspect is more about the maintenance of relationships.

Essential notes

Note that both positive and negative reinforcement make the relationship more likely to occur, just for different reasons. Positive reinforcement is rewarding, whereas negative reinforcement reinforces any behaviour that leads to the avoidance of unpleasant consequences (e.g. rejection or humiliation).

Examiners' notes

When describing this theory in an exam, you should guard against giving too many examples. We have included an example here to make the theory easier to understand, but, when constructing an answer, you should concentrate more on the main psychological claims of the theory.

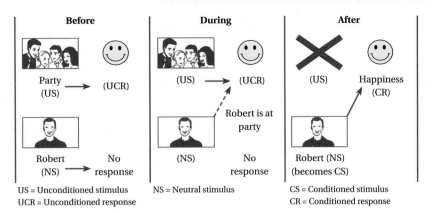

Natalie is in need of cheering up. Her friends invite her to a party.

US = Unconditioned stimulus
UCR = Unconditioned response

NS = Neutral stimulus

CS = Conditioned stimulus
CR = Conditioned response

Fig. 1
The process of classical conditioning in relationship formation

Research supporting the reward/need satisfaction model

The rewarding nature of relationships

In a study using MRI scans, Aron *et al.* (2005) investigated the brain activation of 17 individuals who reported being intensely in love.

- They asked participants to rate how much in love they were.

- It was found that the dopamine-rich areas of the brain associated with reward were activated to a greater extent when individuals were shown a photo of the person with whom they had fallen in love, in contrast to someone who they just liked.

- The amount of activity also correlated with the degree to which they felt in love.

This supports the claim that we form relationships with those people who provide us with rewards; in this case, being in love increases dopamine activity in the brain, which is rewarding.

The effect of classical conditioning on perception of attractiveness

May and Hamilton (1980) conducted an experiment to look at the role that association played in relationship formation.

- Female participants evaluated photographs of men while listening either to rock music that stimulated positive mood, to 'modern' music that stimulated negative mood, or to no music at all.

- The participants gave more positive evaluations of personal character, physical attractiveness and general attraction in the rock music condition than in the other two conditions.

This demonstrates that associating someone with a good feeling (e.g. that the rock music stimulated) can make it more likely they will be attracted to them. However, it should be noted that being *attracted* to someone does not mean that a person would be more likely to form a relationship with them. Other factors (such as matching, opportunity and so on) would determine whether a relationship would be initiated.

This topic continues on the next spread. ☛

Evaluation of the reward/need satisfaction model

Overemphasis on reward

Reward is not as powerful a predictor of the formation of relationships as originally thought, as many relationships, such as parent/child relationships, do not seem to be driven by the need for reinforcement. This suggests, therefore, that rewards may not be fundamentally important in the formation of intimate relationships. In this case rewards are more long-term rather than immediate. This makes sense from an evolutionary perspective, as the formation of long-lasting intimate relationships makes the care of children easier, providing 'rewards' at the genetic level for both parents.

Not all rewards prompt relationship formation

One form of reward is argued by evolutionary psychologists to be sexual access. If good feelings are associated with relationship formation, then it would be expected that if someone has sexual intercourse with another person, this would be rewarding enough to prompt formation of a relationship. This is not the case. One-night stands and the use of prostitutes are testament to this, highlighting the fact that sex alone is not a strong enough reward to prompt formation of a relationship – there is more complexity in the process.

Remote relationships weaken the association element of this theory

Classical conditioning is less likely to occur if the person is not present; therefore, the formation of long-distance and **cyber relationships** (i.e. relationships formed over the Internet) challenges the view that all relationships are formed on the basis of 'attraction through association'. However, it could be argued that other rewards may be present in cyber relationships (e.g. the rewards of similar attitudes and mutual disclosure) that outweigh the association element of attraction in the formation of these relationships.

Evaluation using research

Fairness is underestimated

Perhaps we're not as selfish as the reward/need satisfaction model suggests? Hays' (1985) work examining friendships seems to indicate that we are concerned with fairness for both parties (equity), not just maximizing our own rewards. He stated that a degree of mutual liking is important for friendship formation, yet the reward/need satisfaction model does not focus on reciprocity, but more on personal reward (i.e. what one person can get out of a relationship).

Essential notes

Evolutionary theorists might argue that because relationships make reproduction and the care of children easier, being in a relationship provides long-term rewards for both partners. They propose various **adaptive** mechanisms to bring this about, such as the rewarding feelings of 'falling in love'.

Essential notes

Most research in this area has focused on the development of face-to-face romantic relationships. However, we live in a changing world, where relationships are also formed, maintained and even terminated over the Internet or phone. The rewards offered by such relationships may not be immediately evident, but that does not mean they do not exist.

Rewards are not always important

Aron *et al.* (1989) gathered accounts of falling in love from 522 participants using questionnaires and written accounts. They then compared them to accounts of forming friendships. They found that there was relatively little support for the idea that relationship formation is dependent on rewards. Indeed, the major determinants seem to be being liked and desirable characteristics such as a pleasant personality and good looks. While this does not contradict the theory, it places greater emphasis on the direct reinforcement (reward) aspect of 'feeling good', rather then a long-term fulfilment of needs.

Issues, debates and approaches (IDA)

Gender and cultural differences

Cross-cultural and gender research highlights that the rewards associated with relationships vary between cultures and genders. Women may be socialized into putting their needs as secondary to others, as demanded by the society in which they live. This then, in terms of the theory, would see the reward mechanism for some women as different – not only from the men in their cultures, but also from the women of other cultures. Their reward might not be how much they personally gain, but more how much they are seen as caring for others (Lott 1994). This suggests a cultural and gender bias to the theory, with some psychologists suggesting that the theory applies mainly to Western cultures, where the pursuit of personal happiness is more important in the formation of personal relationships than it is in other cultures.

Deterministic

This theory may be considered **deterministic** because it suggests that when others provide us with reinforcement or are in some way associated with reinforcement, relationships are more likely to form with those individuals. The implication, therefore, is that in the absence of such reinforcement, relationships will *not* form. In other words, when it comes to the formation (or not) of relationships, our behaviour is *determined* by the likelihood of reinforcement. The fact that there is conflicting evidence (see the Hays study described earlier) would challenge the deterministic view that our main aim is to seek reward for ourselves when forming relationships.

Ethnocentric

The theory can be criticized as being **ethnocentric. Collectivist cultures** do not have the same emphasis on the need for reward and satisfaction of the individual. It should be noted that helping others and self-sacrificing can be a reward in itself, so this may drive formation of a relationship rather than personal reward. Arranged marriages are not based on positive associations made through conditioning, and their formation is for less emotional reasons (e.g. family ties, financial reasons).

Examiners' notes

It is important always to 'use' studies such as this in an evaluative way, i.e. by identifying a critical point and then using the research study to reinforce that point. Make it obvious whether it is supporting or challenging a point of view. Merely describing a study that may be relevant to the area does not constitute AO2 evaluation unless you use it in this way. The 'Strong answers' in the exam section good give examples of how to use research in this way. See p. 52, for example, where research by Dunbar (1995) is used to build an effective commentary.

Examiners' notes

There is a requirement for discussion of issues, debates and approaches (IDA) when answering questions about relationships. You will receive some credit for illustrating gender or cultural *differences*, but you will receive *more* credit if you use this information to build a point about how this creates a cultural (or gender) *bias* in the theory or study. This is important because it means there is a more fundamental problem of interpretation of the theory rather than just some interesting points about differences in how people behave. You will find several examples of how IDA commentary can be integrated successfully into essays in the Exam section. See, for example, p. 52 (fourth paragraph, on gender bias) and p. 55 (first paragraph, on cultural bias).

The matching hypothesis

The emphasis of the **matching hypothesis** is that couples seek to form relationships with the best possible partner they think they can attract. They also want to feel that they have the best possible partner that won't reject *them*. As a consequence of this, it is observed that people who form couples have similar levels of attractiveness. The 'matching hypothesis' has two specific hypotheses:

1. The more socially desirable a person is (e.g. in terms of physical attractiveness), the more desirable they would expect their partner to be.
2. Couples who are matched in terms of their **social desirability** are more likely to have a happy relationship than are couples who are mismatched.

The importance of physical attractiveness

If someone is seen to be physically attractive, then they are thought to have other positive attributes as well, such as being more sociable, more skilled in social situations and perhaps even more sexually accessible, despite there being no initial information to suggest these attributes. This is known as the **'halo effect'** and highlights that physical attractiveness is important in relationship formation.

Other considerations

This does not mean simply that physical attractiveness is the only determinant of choice of partner, as *social* attractiveness is also considered. Attributes such as status, wealth and popularity are also included in the decision about forming a relationship. It is acknowledged, however, that initially physical attractiveness is the first determinant as it is the easiest to judge. People do not just take into account what they think they want in a partner, but also the likelihood of that person feeling similarly and therefore accepting any attempt to form a relationship. No one likes to be turned down!

The computer dance study

Walster's computer dance study (Walster *et al.* 1966) tested the matching hypothesis by inviting university students to a 'get acquainted' dance. Each student was asked to complete a questionnaire so that a suitable partner could be picked for them (they had been already surreptitiously rated for physical attractiveness by a group of researchers). In fact, the pairing was done randomly. They were introduced to their 'date' and spent time with them at the dance. At the end of the evening, they were asked to evaluate their partner and to comment on whether they would like to meet up with them again.

The researchers found that, regardless of their own level of physical attractiveness, participants reacted more positively to physically attractive dates and were more likely to try to arrange subsequent dates with them. In this study the 'physical attractiveness effect' was greater than any 'matching effect' or any concerns about rejection.

In 1969, Walster carried out an extension to this study, but this time she ensured that participants had time to mix before the event so that they had time to meet 'naturally', (thus making the study closer to real-life conditions). The results of this study supported the matching hypothesis, in that participants paired up with people who were perceived by researchers (as well perhaps as themselves) to be of a similar level of attractiveness.

Murstein's 'faces study' (1972)

Murstein also conducted a study that supports the matching hypothesis. He showed photographs of the faces of 'steady or engaged' couples (i.e. 'real' couples) to participants, along with some pictures of 'random' couples put together for the purposes of the experiment. The real couples were judged consistently to be more similar to each other in terms of physical attractiveness than were the random couples. Murstein claimed that the findings of the study showed that individuals with equal ratings for physical attractiveness are more likely to form an intimate relationship rather than individuals who differed in terms of physical attractiveness.

The Murstein study is useful because the participants were real-life couples rather than couples formed by the contrived and potentially artificial setting of Walster's dance. This is important because the decision-making (by the partners) will also have been *realistic*, lending support to the matching hypothesis (as did the later Walster study). The original Walster study, in contrast, found that decision-making was *optimistic*, in that the most attractive students were also the ones who most people wanted to meet up with again.

This topic continues on the next spread. ☞

Examiners' notes

When describing a research study in the exam, there is no need to include all this detail. You should pick out the main findings and any conclusions to illustrate how these relate to the predictions of the theory. This takes practice, so that is very much down to you!

Examiners' notes

Remember the golden rule if you want to use research studies such as these as part of your AO2 evaluation. They *must* be built into a critical argument that evaluates the matching hypothesis – don't just describe the study and leave it to the examiner to work out the relevance.

Evaluation of the matching hypothesis

The consideration of physical attractiveness

The focus on attraction in the matching hypothesis may derive from the kinds of environment where people are thought to meet. Dances, parties, loud bars, etc., are popular places to meet a partner; in such settings the only real information you can get about a potential partner is their level of physical attractiveness.

This may explain why such emphasis has been placed on physical attractiveness in research. This does not challenge the theory, as it is likely that someone judges social attractiveness on the information available – if only physical information is available, then the judgement must be made on that information.

Complex matching

The original matching hypothesis proposed that people tend to pair up with others of similar social desirability, and the concept of social desirability has become synonymous with physical attractiveness alone. However, this is a very narrow definition of 'desirability', and research (e.g. Whelan and Boxer 2008) suggests that people come into a relationship offering many desirable characteristics, perhaps compensating for a lack of physical attractiveness with an attractive personality, status, money and so on.

Research support

Huston (1973) conducted a study that examined whether the possibility of rejection played any part in the process of formation of relationships. Men were shown pictures of women who had previously been rated for their physical attractiveness and were asked to say which one they would prefer to date. Huston found that men were likely to choose attractive women, but only if they felt they were not going to be rejected. This supports one of the central claims of the matching hypothesis – that is, that likelihood of rejection plays a part in the decision to initiate a relationship.

An alternative view: the reward/need satisfaction theory

The reward/need satisfaction theory (see pp. 4–7) proposes that there is a complexity in the process of partner choice that the matching hypothesis does not emphasize. According to this view, people select partners not because they are matched in terms of social desirability, but because they offer rewards or satisfy needs. However, the two theories are not in opposition as the reward/need satisfaction theory does suggest that more socially desirable individuals are also more rewarding.

Essential notes

Matching, it appears, is usually thought of in terms of physical attractiveness alone. However, matching may also be in terms of a range of other characteristics, some obvious and some not so obvious.

Examiners' notes

When including a study as part of your evaluation, be sure to make it clear what particular aspect of a theory is supported (or challenged) by the study. It isn't sufficient simply to point out that a study 'supports the theory', because usually a study focuses on testing just one aspect of a particular theory. Huston's theory supports the claim that 'fear of rejection' is one of the driving influences of the matching process.

Issues, debates and approaches (IDA)

Gender differences

Takeuchi (2006) has shown that a gender difference exists in how far physical attractiveness is valued by an opposite-sex partner. Physical attractiveness of women appears to be valued more heavily by men, but physical attractiveness of men is valued less by women and so has less of an impact on women's perception of the social desirability of men. This suggests that men can more easily compensate for a lack of physical attractiveness by displaying other desirable characteristics, such as kindness and generosity.

There are also 'within-gender' differences in terms of how far attractiveness (as opposed to other other characteristics) affects decision-making. Towhey (1979) found that individuals who scored high on the gender stereotypical scale were more likely to make their decision based on physical attractiveness.

An evolutionary perspective

Buss and Shackelford (2008) offer an evolutionary explanation for gender differences in matching 'standards'. They found that women typically look for mates who have a range of 'desirable characteristics', such as good genes (e.g. masculine), good investment (e.g. resources), good partner (e.g. kindness) and good parenting characteristics. Most women must usually compromise and so may select partners who possess some, rather than all of, these desirable characteristics; in other words, they must match *their* 'mate value' to that of a potential partner. However, claim Buss and Shackelford, attractive women have high mate value and so are more likely to demand a mate who possesses all the desirable characteristics rather than matching simply on the basis of physical attractiveness.

Matching as a reductionist concept

The matching hypothesis simplifies the formation of relationships and could therefore be seen to be **reductionist**. It states that the formation of a relationship can be 'reduced' to just two factors: the best possible partner and the best possible non-rejecting partner. No attention is paid to factors such as proximity (i.e. who is available and 'nearby') and other factors such as complementarity of needs.

This seemingly contradictory view suggests that people are sometimes drawn to opposites – for example, a 'weak' person is attracted to a 'strong' person: someone with a need to be looked after is drawn to someone who is a 'looker-afterer'!

Essential notes

This represents a gender bias in the matching process. Physical attractiveness is more highly valued by men, and therefore has a greater influence on what they appear to regard as the 'best possible partner'. Research suggests this is not the case for women who consider other factors as more important when determining *their* 'best possible partner'.

Essential notes

Reductionism is usually thought of as being equivalent to *physiological* reductionism, but in fact can refer to any attempt to reduce a complex phenomenon (such as the formation of relationships) down to just one factor (e.g. the need for matching).

'Economic theories' of relationship maintenance

Economic theories of relationship maintenance are based on the idea that we look at our relationships in the same way as we do a business deal. Two theories based on this notion are social exchange theory and equity theory.

Social exchange theory

Essential notes

At the centre of this theory is the belief that people invest resources in a partner (their time, commitment and resources) with the expectation that they will earn a profit as a result of this 'investment'.

Social exchange theory claims that, for the individual, the best result from a relationship would be to make a profit; for this to occur, there must be minimum cost and maximum reward. The principles of operant conditioning apply in this theory. If something is rewarding, we pursue and value it. On the other hand, if something is costly, we avoid it as we would avoid punishment. Examples of 'rewards' would include gaining a partner with good looks, money, and loyalty. In terms of cost, a person would take into account obvious costs such as time spent with the partner's family, but also the less obvious costs such as less time being spent with their own friends.

Rewards minus costs equals the outcomes of a relationship. Commitment to a relationship is dependent on the 'profitability' of this outcome. This theory also allows us to predict the outcome of a relationship. If someone has more costs than rewards, then they will probably end the relationship.

Thibaut and Kelley's four-stage model

Thibaut and Kelley (1959) proposed a four-stage model of relationships, illustrating how rewards and costs are explored and established in long-term relationships (see Table 1).

Table 1
Thibaut and Kelley's four-stage model of long-term relationships

1. Sampling	The couple explores the rewards and costs in a variety of relationships.
2. Bargaining	The couple 'costs out' the relationship and identifies the sources of profit and loss.
3. Commitment	The couple settles into a relationship; the exchange of rewards becomes relatively predictable.
4. Institutionalization	The interactions are established; the couple have settled down.

Source: Adapted from Thibaut and Kelley (1959)

Comparison levels

Thibaut and Kelley introduced two comparison levels against which an existing relationship can be evaluated. These enable an individual to judge the 'value' of a current relationship against previous and future relationships.

- The **comparison level** is a comparison between the current (i.e. reference) relationship and what we have been used to in the past or believe is appropriate in the current relationship. If the reference relationship compares favourably, the person is motivated to stay in the relationship.
- The **comparison level for alternatives** is concerned with the benefits of possible alternative relationships, i.e. an alternative partner may offer more positive outcomes. If the person feels they might do better with a new partner, they may end the current relationship.

Equity theory

Despite the fact that many of the main assumptions of exchange theory were supported by research, it soon became clear that, for most people, profit was less important than *fairness* in relationships. This resulted in a modified version of exchange theory – **equity theory** (Walster *et al.* 1978).

Unlike social exchange theory, which states that individuals try to maximize their rewards and minimize their costs, equity theory holds that it is *inequity* (unfairness) in relationships that has the greater potential to create dissatisfaction. People who contribute a great deal in a relationship and receive little in return would perceive inequity, as would those who *receive* a great deal and give little in return.

Walster and colleagues suggested four principles that underpin equity:

1. As suggested by the earlier social exchange theory, people try to *maximize their rewards* in a relationship.
2. *Trading rewards* between both parties occurs to ensure fairness, e.g. a 'favour' or 'privilege' for one partner is paid back by an equivalent 'favour' or 'privilege' for the other partner.
3. *Inequity produces dissatisfaction*, with the person who receives the lower level of reward (the 'loser') experiencing the greater dissatisfaction.
4. The loser will endeavour to rectify the situation, and the greater the perceived inequity, the greater the effort to remedy the situation.

Research on equity and relationship satisfaction

Stafford and Canary (2006) asked over 200 couples to complete measures of equity and marital satisfaction. Satisfaction was highest for spouses who perceived their relationships to be equitable and lowest for partners who considered themselves to be relatively underbenefited. These findings are consistent with the predictions of equity theory.

This topic continues on the next spread. ☞

Essential notes

Although still concerned with gaining rewards from a relationship, individuals are also concerned that rewards should be 'equitable' (i.e. fair) within a relationship. Rewards without equity lead to dissatisfaction.

Examiners' notes

The social exchange and equity theories are collectively economic theories and can be used either together or independently. Make this clear in your answers.

Evaluation of social exchange theory

Research support

Simpson *et al.* (1990) investigated how people deal with the threat of potential alternatives (comparison for alternatives, see p. 13). They asked participants to rate members of the opposite sex in terms of their physical attractiveness and found that those participants who were already involved in a relationship gave lower ratings. This had the effect of lowering the perceived profits associated with a potential new partner and so reducing any threat to their existing relationship.

Social exchange theory: issues, debates and approaches (IDA)

Abusive relationships

Rusbult and Martz (1995) argue that the principles of social exchange can be used to explain why some women stay in abusive relationships. When investments are high (e.g. in terms of children, financial security) and alternatives are relatively low (e.g. lack of money, having nowhere to live), then even an abusive relationship may be regarded as a 'profitable' one, and the woman may then be motivated to stay in that relationship.

Culture bias

Moghaddam (1998) suggests that 'economic' theories such as the social exchange and equity theories only apply to Western cultures and even then only to certain types of relationship among individuals with high social mobility. Less mobile groups and members of many non-Western cultures would be more likely to value security in a relationship than personal profit.

Evaluation of equity theory

Not all couples apply the principle of equity

It appears that some couples do operate on the principle of equity whereas others do not. Research by Clark and Mills (1979) suggested that some couples also work 'communally'. This means that they want to love and care for each other; they do not see their relationship as a situation where they have to give and receive in equal amounts.

It seems that such couples do not keep count of investment and cost, but have the underlying conviction that it will all be even in the end. They are, therefore, happy to accept there may be times when one partner needs more support and does less.

Examiners' notes

Remember that all Unit 3 questions carry a requirement to include material related to issues, debates and approaches (IDA). This will not be stated in the question, but will be a key factor when an examiner awards marks for the AO2/AO3 component of your answer (see pp. 45–7).

Gender differences in responses to inequity

It seems that inequity is perceived differently by the genders. Women are more likely to have extra-marital affairs if they think that their relationship is inequitable and that they are the 'loser'. Indeed, many report that they have had extra-marital affairs for just this reason. This is not the case for males, however, for whom extra-marital affairs tend to be purely sexual in nature, rather than linked to marital satisfaction (Atwater *et al.* 1985).

An invalid explanation of real-life relationships

Feeney *et al.* (1994) argue that equity is not as important in real-life relationships as this theory suggests. Relationships in the modern world are more sophisticated, and a simple cost/benefit analysis is too simplistic. The research that has been conducted on this theory tends to be rather contrived and misses the sophistication of human relationships. Ragsdale and Brandau-Brown (2007) suggest, therefore, that long-term relationships do not work on the equity principle and that the reason people stay together is more complex.

Equity theory: issues, debates and approaches (IDA)

Cultural differences in the importance of equity

Research does not support the view that equity is equally important in all cultures, implying that the equity theory represents a culturally biased view of the factors that are important in relationship satisfaction. Aumer-Ryan *et al.* (2007) interviewed men and women at the University of Hawaii (a relatively individualist culture) and the University of the West Indies in Jamaica (a relatively collectivist culture). They found a cultural difference in how men and women from these different cultures reacted to perceived inequities in their relationships. The Hawaiian sample were most satisfied when they perceived their relationships as equitable, but the Jamaican sample were most satisfied when they perceived themselves to be overbenefiting from their relationship. For both men and women in the Jamaican sample, equity was of less importance in determining relationship satisfaction.

Applications to marital therapy

Research (Larsson *et al.* 1998) has established that wives, compared to husbands, are more likely to feel distressed as a result of perceived inequity in their relationships. It also appears that this inequity affects wives' intimacy with their husbands more than it does husbands' intimacy with their wives. As a result, wives reported lower levels of compatibility when they perceived their relationships to be inequitable. As compatibility is a key factor determining success in marital relationships, this has important implications for couples receiving marital therapy. It suggests that attempts to resolve compatibility issues between a husband and wife are doomed to failure unless issues associated with inequity are addressed first.

Investment theory

Investment theory, instead of concentrating solely on satisfaction in relationships, focuses on the extent to which commitment is determined by *investment*. Rusbult (1983) argued that if someone has invested a great deal in a relationship, then they will have a greater commitment level to the relationship and in making it work. Investments in relationships can be:

- financial – such as a house, gifts, shared possessions
- temporal – time spent together or with the other person's family or friends
- emotional – the welfare of children and shared friends.

Commitment

Commitment is a very important part of the investment model, reflecting each partner's desire to remain in the relationship and their feelings of attachment towards it. In response to threats to the relationship, individuals examine their relationship in terms of three factors:

- *Satisfaction* – As with social exchange and equity theory, satisfaction is the product of rewards/costs equation. If the outcomes of a relationship are acceptable to both parties (i.e. perceived as equitable), then the relationship will be deemed as fair and a greater investment made by both partners.
- *Quality of alternatives* – If available potential partners are no better than the current partner, then the individual will continue to invest in their current relationship.
- *Investment* – If an individual has already invested heavily in a relationship, then they will put more effort into maintaining it. Existing investments can thus have an influence on future commitment, to the extent that a person stays in a poor relationship simply because they have already invested significantly in it.

These three factors determine how committed an individual is to their relationship. Higher levels of satisfaction and investment coupled with lower levels of desired alternatives are predicted to correlate positively with commitment, as shown in Fig. 2.

Fig. 2

The relationship between satisfaction, quality of alternatives and investment in a relationship

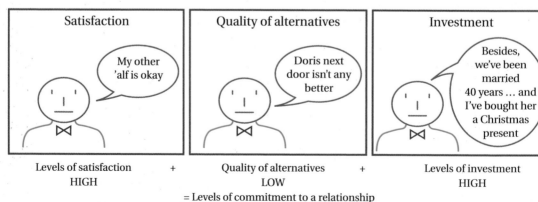

Levels of commitment and responses to relationship problems

An individual's commitment level will determine how they respond to any threats to their relationship. Committed individuals are more likely than others to remain in their relationship and engage in constructive responses to any relationship problems. Committed people also tend to downplay the attractiveness of alternatives, make sacrifices for the sake of the relationship, and believe that their relationship is superior to other people's relationships. Less committed individuals tend to have the opposite reactions to problems (Rusbult *et al.* 1994).

Research on investment theory

Rusbult (1980) tested the investment model in a role-playing study that varied both the size of an individual's investment to a relationship and the quality of potential alternative partners. Rusbult found that commitment to relationships increased with the size of an individual's investment and decreased with the quality of alternatives. This study demonstrated that *both* investment *and* quality of alternatives are influential in the maintenance of relationships.

Rusbult (1983) carried out a further study with college students over seven months, asking them:

- how satisfied they were in their current relationship
- if there were available alternatives (i.e. other potential partners) of good quality
- how much effort and investment they had put into their current relationship.

She found that level of investment and satisfaction were the best predictors for commitment to the relationship.

Dindia and Baxter (1987) looked at how 50 married couples maintained their relationships and increased their marital satisfaction. The interesting finding, that supported the investment model, was that the longer a couple had been together, the fewer strategies they needed to maintain the relationship. This indicates that satisfaction increases with time, and that the greater the temporal investment, the stronger the relationship appears to be.

Impett *et al.* (2005) tested the investment model of relationship commitment and stability using data from both partners of 3 627 married couples. As predicted by the theory, spouses' satisfaction, investment, and quality of alternatives predicted their commitment to the marital relationship. Additionally, the level of commitment assessed at the initial testing stage predicted the likelihood of either marital breakdown or stability 18 months later.

Essential notes

Commitment is not the end-product of the process of relationship maintenance. Commitment merely makes it more likely that individuals will respond positively when faced with relationship difficulties.

Examiners' notes

Although coverage of the studies here is at a descriptive level only, they could be used as part of your AO2 evaluation by adding a few well-chosen evaluative phrases. For example, you might introduce a study by adding 'The claims of the investment model are supported by…' and then demonstrate what specific claims are supported by the theory and why.

This topic continues on the next spread. ☞

Evaluation of investment theory

The components are not independent

Rusbult's model involves three components, and there is an argument that they are not truly independent from each other, as the model suggests. For example, satisfaction may be expressed by somebody in a relationship, but that satisfaction may derive mainly from the fact that they have a lot invested in the relationship. This is an effect that can be explained in terms of **cognitive dissonance**, the presence of two conflicting thoughts or cognitions.

In this example, an individual may have spent a lot of time with their partner, but may actually be dissatisfied with the relationship. This makes them feel bad, so in an effort to feel better, they may convince themselves and others that they really are satisfied. In other words, they change one of the cognitions (e.g. convince themselves they are really satisfied), and so make the two cognitions consistent again.

Research support

A **meta-analysis** by Le and Agnew (2003) supports the main predictions of the investment model. Across 52 studies, they found that satisfaction with, alternatives to, and investments in a relationship were related significantly with commitment in the relationship. The three variables together accounted for nearly 66 per cent of the variance in commitment within relationships. Commitment, in turn, often accurately predicted the likelihood of relationship break-up.

Le and Agnew also found gender differences in the relationship between these factors and commitment to relationships. Women were more satisfied with their relationship, felt that they had invested more in the relationship and perceived fewer alternatives to the current relationship.

Problems with the investment construct

Sprecher (1988) argued that investment does not directly predict commitment to a relationship. In a survey, she tested the predictions that satisfaction, investments and social support predicted commitment, while quality of alternatives and inequity decrease commitment.

The findings generally supported these predictions, except that the role of investments was not significant. Sprecher claimed that Rusbult had included the investment construct without any reference to important social support variables (such as family and friends). Sprecher concluded that satisfaction and alternatives were the more important factors in determining commitment.

Investment model versus social exchange/equity

Social exchange theory examines satisfaction in relationships in terms of how much reward there is. Its later hybrid – equity theory – looked at satisfaction too in terms of fairness. Rusbult's theory does not contradict these theories; it merely extends it to include quality of alternatives and investment.

A study by Michaels *et al.* (1986) researched both social exchange/equity theories and the investment model. Their main focus was to consider what the greatest determinants of commitment were. They tested the idea that relationship commitment is influenced by:

- relationship outcomes (as in social exchange and equity theories)
- outcomes relative to the attractiveness of alternatives
- relationship satisfaction and duration (as suggested by investment theory).

They used self-report data from college students dating one person exclusively and found strong support for all the factors as affecting commitment levels.

Issues, debates and approaches (IDA)

Cultural bias

It may be argued that the investment model reflects an ethnocentric bias as an explanation of people's commitment to relationships. Cross-culturally, satisfaction, quality of alternatives and investment are not always factors that influence commitment to a relationship. There may be cultural or religious pressures to maintain a relationship, and in some cultures, relationship break-up, especially of a marriage, is not socially accepted. Alternatively, it may be less acceptable for one gender rather than the other to initiate a relationship break-up based on these considerations.

Attachment styles and the investment model

Pistole *et al.* (1995) examined the relationship between adult attachment styles and Rusbult's investment model of relationships. Responses from 239 participants indicated that those who are securely attached experience greater satisfaction, fewer costs and greater commitment in their relationships than did those who had an anxious or avoidant attachment style. The highest costs were reported by anxious individuals, while avoidant types reported the lowest investments. Pistole and colleagues concluded that secure attachment is associated with greater commitment to current relationships, while insecure attachment – particularly avoidant – is associated with less commitment.

Investment and abusive relationships

Rusbult's investment model is used to understand the conditions under which individuals are likely to remain in abusive relationships. Rusbult and Martz (1995) interviewed women at a shelter for battered women. They found that when abused women felt their investment in a relationship was significant (for example, they had been together for a long time or had children together), they were less likely to leave their partners. Consistent with the predictions of the model, feelings of commitment were greater among women who:

- had relatively poor-quality economic alternatives
- had invested more heavily in their relationships (e.g. were married rather than in a casual relationship)
- experienced lesser dissatisfaction (e.g. reported less severe abuse).

Examiners' notes

Comparing one theory with another can be a valuable way of earning AO2 marks. This is done particularly effectively here through a research study, so would earn appropriate credit through elaboration of the initial idea (that is, that investment and social exchange/equity theories do not necessarily contradict each other).

Examiners' notes

It is important to retain the relevance of any material to the model being evaluated. In this case, we have examined the link between the investment model and attachment styles. This is not an invitation to get carried away describing other characteristics of secure and insecurely attached adults.

Models of relationship breakdown

Duck's original model

Initially, Duck (1982) suggested a four-stage model of relationship breakdown that couples went through whilst splitting up. Duck's four stages were:

- The 'intrapsychic' stage – brooding about negative aspects of the relationship
- The 'dyadic' stage – confronting the partner with any resulting dissatisfaction
- The 'social' stage – involving others, as the partners 'go public' with their relationship problems and must now sort out what happens next
- The 'grave-dressing' stage – each partner relating to others their own version of why the relationship failed.

A model of relationship breakdown (Rollie and Duck 2006)

Duck's theory was later refined (Rollie and Duck 2006) and further aspects were added. Unlike the earlier model, the model focuses on the *processes* (e.g. patterns of communication) that typify relationship breakdown, rather than focusing on distinct stages that people must pass through. Each of the processes in the model has different purposes and ultimately different consequences.

Essential notes

The fact that the 2006 model is refined from the earlier model could be used as evaluation to state that it takes into account recent research and is therefore a better model than before.

Examiners' notes

Use Fig. 3 to help your memory. Each of the six cartoons represents one phase of the breakdown process and illustrates what happens within that phase.

Fig. 3

The six processes in Rollie and Duck's (2006) refined model of relationship breakdown

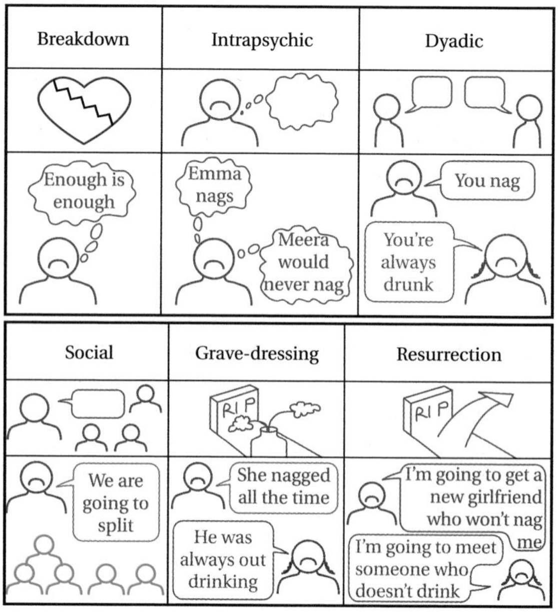

An outline of the six processes in Rollie and Duck's model is given below.

Breakdown
The turning point or threshold for this element is when one party in the relationship reaches a point when they consider that the relationship should finish. If things do not improve, and the dissatisfaction is great enough, they will move to the next phase.

Intrapsychic processes
An individual who has reached the breakdown point looks hard at their relationship and may see the other partner in negative terms. This promotes a social withdrawal, so that the individual can nurse their wounds, taking stock of their position and their dissatisfaction with the relationship. At this point, grievances have not yet been aired; more thinking than communicating occurs.

Dyadic processes
These processes begin once the person declares their resentment to the partner. The perceived problems are then aired and disputed by the partners. The relationship can be saved by effective communication and a resolve on the part of both parties to address the problems they are experiencing. However, it can also highlight the weaknesses within the relationship. In this instance, the relationship break-up could move on to the point where a split is announced.

Social processes
Now the intention to break up the relationship is made public. There will be advice from relatives and friends to listen to, which may perhaps mend the relationship or delay its conclusion. It is also the time when each partner justifies the break-up, sometimes placing the blame on the other person. The longer this stage goes on, the more likely that the couple will split.

Grave-dressing processes
The split has usually already occurred when these processes begin. It is when the 'official' account of the split is formulated by those involved. Of course, it does not necessarily mean that both accounts are the same; indeed, they often differ. Grave-dressing processes are important in terms of making sure that their account of the split does not deter potential new partners by putting themselves in a good light.

Resurrection processes
We might describe someone in the resurrection stage as 'picking themselves up, dusting themselves down and starting all over again'. It is the point when someone moves on, possibly to another relationship. They also learn from their previous mistakes and think about what they want in future in a relationship. The newly single partners may now believe that 'this time everything will be different'.

This topic continues on the next spread. ☞

Examiners' notes

You will never be asked to provide this much descriptive detail about a model of relationship breakdown – you should, therefore, practise précising the content on this page into about 200 to 240 words to preserve the gist of the model. When answering questions on relationship breakdown, it would be perfectly acceptable (indeed advisable) to concentrate solely on the Rollie and Duck model.

Evaluation of Rollie and Duck's model

Advantage over traditional stage models

A major problem with traditional 'stage' theories of relationship breakdown is that, in an attempt to reduce breakdown to basic and universal components, there is an inevitable sacrifice of accuracy and usefulness to the management of relationships in real life. As models become more simplistic, they lose their ability to describe these complex processes adequately. Many relational processes are unpredictable and not easily reduced to a simple model. By emphasizing the typical patterns of communication associated with different phases of breakdown rather than a fixed pattern of stages that must proceed in a linear fashion, Rollie and Duck's model offers a more realistic description of how these processes develop in real life.

Positive viewpoint

The resurrection phase represents a positive view of relationship break-ups and highlights the potential for personal growth that a break-up can prompt. As many people do benefit from leaving a relationship, then this would appear to be a realistic addition to the model. Traditional models of breakdown focus primarily on the distress caused by break-ups, rather than on the potential for growth that is represented in this model.

Gender differences

The personal growth discussed in the previous evaluation point appears, however, to be gender specific. Women seem to benefit to a greater extent following the dissolution of a relationship, so it is important that the possibility of personal growth is emphasized rather than the inevitability. Exactly why women benefit is unclear, but it is suggested that the emancipation from a potentially limiting relationship is the cause. Women also report more post-relationship growth than men, possibly due to the greater social support available, although research has shown that increased social support is not necessarily associated with growth. For example, Brock and Lawrence (2009) found that too much informational support (usually in the form of unsolicited advice) was actually worse than no support at all.

The impact of relationship breakdown

Akert (1998) found that the role people played in the decision to end a relationship was the most important predictor of the impact of the breakdown. Akert found that partners who did not initiate the break-up also tended to be the most miserable, reported the highest levels of loneliness and unhappiness after the end of the relationship. However, partners who initiated the break-up found the ending of the relationship less upsetting and less stressful than those who did not.

Issues, debates and approaches (IDA)

An ethnocentric bias

Most research is based on data from White, middle-class individuals and therefore displays an ethnocentric bias. As relationships are affected by the culture in which they form, then social expectations when the relationship breaks down will also affect the process of the break-up. Certainly it could be argued that in a culture where divorce and separation of married couples is frowned upon, the social processes phase will be received differently than in cultures where relationship breakdown is more widely accepted.

Similarly, in cultures where polygamy is practised, the resurrection phase may not apply as individuals have multiple partners already.

A heterosexual bias

A limitation of most of the models of relationship breakdown, including this one, is that they have been developed from the experiences of *heterosexual* individuals. As a result, they may not represent the experiences of other groups such as gay and lesbian partnerships.

Similarly, within heterosexual partnerships, there are many different types of romantic relationship, including married, cohabiting and dating couples.

Given the differences between these types of relationship, as well as the differences in the investments made by the individuals in these relationships, it is unlikely that the processes experienced will be exactly the same.

Real-life application

The model can have real-life applications if used to help prevent breakdown of a relationship. Duck claims that by paying attention to the topics that people discuss and how they talk about their relationship, it may be possible to intervene before the breakdown progresses. This not only offers an indication about their stage in the process, but may also suggest interventions appropriate to that stage. For example:

- An individual in the intrapsychic phase might be encouraged to think about the strengths of their partner and to reflect upon their own contribution to the current problem.
- Individuals who attempt to enlist support from others might be seen as being in the social phase, already committed to leaving and therefore in need of advice about how to do it (e.g. requiring a face-saving way out of the relationship).

Examiners' notes

When making a critical point such as claiming an ethnocentric bias, you should focus the point on the relevant parts of the model (i.e. social processes and resurrection) where this bias is more likely to be evident.

Essential notes

This does not mean that the model is irrelevant in explaining the breakdown of same-sex relationships, but that the circumstances of these relationships may accentuate the importance of certain phases. For example, because of perceived intolerant attitudes, same-sex partners may not make their relationship obvious to members of their social network. As a result, members of the social network may not be in a position to offer social support when the partnership enters the social processes phase. The lower levels of social support offered to many same-sex couples may, therefore, contribute to the likelihood of a break-up.

An evolutionary perspective on relationship breakdown

Relationships have always broken down throughout history. However, there seems to be an advantage, in an evolutionary sense, to staying in a relationship long term. This is because childrearing is more successful when there is a long-term relationship between partners. Mothers who are breast-feeding need a constant supply of food to ensure the quality of their milk and to maintain its production. Through most of history, this was the only option for mothers – hence their reliance on male resources. In a long-term relationship, the mother can expect to be supported by the father and kept well throughout the pregnancy, during childbirth and after the child is born. It also means that there is constant sexual access for both sexes. Being in a relationship, therefore, is **adaptive** – that is, it enhances reproductive **fitness** for both sexes.

Because of this evolutionary advantage, evolutionary theory has predictions about relationship break-up and the reasons behind the apparent differences between the sexes.

Evolutionary theory also suggests reasons behind the behaviour of the person breaking up the relationship (the 'rejector'), and the person with whom they are finishing their relationship (the 'rejectee').

The costs of relationship breakdown

Perilloux and Buss (2008) have developed an explanation of why evolution might have shaped the behaviour of rejectors and rejectees differently. Their research is based on four main predictions.

Prediction 1: Costs related to emotional investment

For women, it may be more costly to lose the stability of a relationship than it is for men. Traditionally, women have been the primary caregivers of children and are, therefore, dependent on resources (such as food and shelter) from the male. From an evolutionary perspective, it is important, then, for women to be in a stable and supportive relationship. This means that women should prefer mates with resources or the potential to acquire resources.

If the male has high emotional investment in a relationship, then he is more likely to share his resources with his partner and family. A breakdown of that relationship could mean that his resources are less freely shared; indeed, he might use his resources in another relationship, leaving his children unsupported. Because of the importance of these resources to the female, female rejectees would experience higher costs associated with losing the emotional investment of their male partner.

Prediction 2: Increasing commitment as a response to the threat of break-up

Women value emotional commitment highly in mates, especially to ensure the survival of any offspring, so males threatened with relationship breakdown may employ strategies to exploit this. They may signal an

Essential notes

There are significant gender differences in what the different sexes look for in a potential mate; it makes sense, therefore, that these basic differences would inform what we might expect to happen when relationships break down.

Examiners' notes

These four predictions constitute an evolutionary explanation of observed gender differences in the impact of relationship breakdown. When planning your answer, you should extract the underlying rationale for these gender differences (this is the AO1 content), which will then be supported (the AO2 content) by research findings on pp. 26–7.

The evolutionary perspective of relationship breakdown suggests that women would experience higher costs if they lose the emotional investment of their partner

Emotional commitment is highly valued by females, so males may use this as a positive inducement to prevent a relationship from breaking down

increase in their commitment (e.g. by suggesting marriage or cohabitation) in order to ensure that a relationship does not finish.

Perilloux and Buss predict this strategy would be less effective when used by females. This is most likely to be due to the fact that it is usually males who provide resources rather than females, which means the emotional commitment of males is more biologically significant than that of females.

Prediction 3: Infidelity

Infidelity may be a deliberate attempt to break up a relationship with a relatively poor-quality mate. This strategy can be used by either partner to break up an existing relationship and thereby free themselves to begin a relationship with a higher-quality mate. However, Perilloux and Buss predict that strategies used by females would be less effective (presumably because males have less invested in the relationship, e.g. don't feel so responsible for care of any children).

Sexual variety, it is suggested by evolutionary theory, is more important to men than women. Infidelity serves this desire by giving the man sexual access to females outside the relationship; it may also help a rejector find a replacement mate quickly following an anticipated break-up. Perilloux and Buss suggest that males are, therefore, more likely than females to engage in sexual activities with new potential mates *prior* to the break-up of an existing relationship. In addition, it is predicted that males would attempt to secure sexual activities with the rejectee *after* the break-up, as this would maximize their reproductive **fitness**.

Prediction 4: Managing reputational damage

Rejectors may be perceived as cruel and heartless by peers (and by potential mates), whereas the rejectee is frequently perceived as the victim. Any reputational damage may adversely affect the chances of the rejector obtaining a long-term mate in the future. For this reason, rejectors will be motivated to minimize any reputational damage and make efforts to be seen as reasonable and compassionate rather than cruel and heartless.

This topic continues on the next spread. ☞

Examiners' notes

Answering exam questions efficiently means responding appropriately to the different demands of questions in this area.

For example, if you were using this material on Perilloux and Buss to answer a question on 'one' explanation of relationship breakdown, the AO1 and AO2 content combined would be about 600–700 words. The AO1 content should make up one-third of this, so you would need approximately 200 to 240 words of description from these two pages for the marks available for AO1. This means a précis of this material down to about half the content given here.

However, if the question asks for 'two' explanations, then this would require just 100 to 120 words on each explanation – in other words, half of your previous précis! In this situation, the Perilloux and Buss (2008) theory could count as one explanation and the Rollie and Duck theory (see pp. 20–3) could count as the other. You should be prepared for both of these questions, and prepare your content accordingly.

Evaluation of research into the evolutionary perspective

Perilloux and Buss (2008) conducted research to test their predictions. They asked 199 heterosexual student participants to complete a questionnaire. All of these participants had experienced at least one break-up, with 80 per cent as the rejector and 71 per cent as the rejectee. Results supported all four predictions as follows.

Prediction 1: Costs related to emotional investment

Perilloux and Buss (2008) predicted that break-ups of relationships cost women more. Women did indeed report more severe emotional responses after break-up and expressed more costliness than did men. Although this finding is consistent with evolutionary predictions, it contradicts the findings based on Rollie and Duck's model that women tend to report more personal growth after break-up (see p. 22).

Prediction 2: Increasing commitment as a response to the threat of break-up

As predicted, Perilloux and Buss found that displays of commitment as a way of preventing a break-up were more effective when used by men than by women.

Prediction 3: Infidelity

As predicted, male rejectors did report engaging in extra-relationship affairs more than female rejectors did. Perilloux and Buss had also predicted that males would attempt to secure additional activities with the rejectee after the break-up. However, they found no evidence of gender differences in this behaviour. They found evidence that women were also often likely to engage in post-break-up sexual activities with the former partner. It is possible that this is because gender differences are less pronounced at this age or in the student environment, as there are numerous opportunities at a university for sexual access to other mates. Women may also engage in sexual activities with their former mate in an attempt to re-establish the relationship.

Prediction 4: Managing reputational damage

Findings suggest that rejectors fear being seen as cruel and heartless, and so use strategies to avoid acquiring this reputation. The most successful way of doing this appeared to be by helping to boost the self-esteem of the rejectee. The findings supported this idea, showing that rejectors were more likely to attempt to boost their ex-partner's self-esteem than were rejectees.

Limitations of the Perilloux and Buss study

A limited sample

This study was limited in using a fairly narrow age range of participants – heterosexual college students. Limiting the sample to just heterosexual participants tells us nothing about the process of relationship breakdown in same-sex couples, where reproductive factors are not an issue. Older individuals may well face quite different adaptive problems following break-up, involving shared children and shared resources. The presence of children would make any break-up more costly to both partners because of the loss of bi-parental care and investment.

The limitations of self-report

Data were acquired using self-reports of their experiences from the student participants. Perilloux and Buss suggest that it would be better to include other data sources, such as reports from close friends or the romantic partners themselves to supplement the self-reports of the participants.

Limitations of the evolutionary perspective

The adaptive benefits of flexible minds

The claim that human behaviour is influenced by adaptations that developed in the Stone Age makes sense only if the environmental challenges remain static over evolutionary time. However, if the environment, including the social environment, is dynamic rather than static (which evidence suggests is the case), then the only human mind that would be adaptive is one that is flexible and responsive in whatever social and physical environment it finds itself. In some environments, it might be adaptive for males and females to act in the ways suggested by Perilloux and Buss, but not in all. This challenges the claim of these being universal human behaviours.

Issues, debates and approaches (IDA)

Ultimate or proximate causes?

Critics have pointed out that characteristics that have been considered universal often turn out to be dependent on cultural and/or historical circumstances. Nichols (1985) argues that explanations based on the adaptive problems faced by our distant ancestors (i.e. **ultimate causes**) neglect important **proximate causes**. For example, research (e.g. Gibbons 1995) has demonstrated important cultural differences in the way relationships are viewed and enacted, and also in the way that men and women in different cultures deal with the loss of a mate. These differences are attributed to local customs and traditions rather than the adaptive problems faced by early humans.

Gender bias

Hollway (1989) argues that the gender differences evident in the relationship behaviour of males and females reflect less the role of evolutionary forces and more the shared **cultural discourses** of the different sexes. These discourses are patterns of thinking and communication that are common within one gender but not the other within a particular culture. For example, with the 'male sexual drive' discourse, a man may be more likely to report greater infidelity (as was the case in the Perilloux and Buss study), yet Hollway claims this is not because he is like that 'by nature', but because there is a cultural discourse that instructs him how to act on the basis of his sex. As a result, evolutionary explanations of sex differences in this area represent a gender-biased representation of how males and females behave during relationship break-ups.

Examiners' notes

To be able to access marks in the top mark bands you need to include some discussion of IDA. Try to avoid simply adding a disjointed paragraph or two at the end of an essay – instead, build these points into the structure of your essay.

Essential notes

Gender differences in how individuals react to relationship breakdown may be less determined by our adaptive biology and more to do with what males and females believe is the appropriate way to behave given that they are products of gender-specific socialization within that particular society.

Sexual selection and human reproductive behaviour

The nature of sexual selection

Evolutionary explanations of human reproductive behaviour are based on the principles of **sexual selection**, a view that competition for mates between individuals of the same sex affects the evolution of certain traits.

Sexual selection and reproductive success

According to sexual selection theory, if a particular characteristic (e.g. youthfulness or body shape) becomes established as a universal preference among males, then females with that characteristic will have greater chance of reproductive success, and these characteristics will become increasingly exaggerated over evolutionary time. Buss (1989) investigated the mate preferences of human males and found that males in most cultures regarded the female 'hourglass' shape as particularly attractive. In terms of sexual selection theory, this is logical because this shape is an indicator of fertility in women (Workman and Reader 2008).

Sexual selection is sometimes at odds with natural selection, however, in that a characteristic that increases an individual's chances of reproductive success may also inhibit their chances of survival. A good example of this is the peacock's tail, which makes the male more attractive to the female but is cumbersome and more conspicuous to predators.

Intrasexual and intersexual selection

- Males must compete with other males for access to mates, and this leads to **intrasexual selection** (selection *within* the same sex).
- Females make a greater investment in their offspring and so must take care to choose the best-quality mate. As there is usually no shortage of males, this leads to **intersexual selection** (selection *between* the sexes).

The origins of mate choice

According to evolutionary theory, human mate preferences were formed in the **environment of evolutionary adaptiveness (EEA)**, sometime between 10 000 and five million years ago. These preferences have been passed on to modern-day females through evolved neural adaptations that favour mating with individuals who possess these desirable traits. Knowing that the genetic quality of a mate will determine the genetic quality of any offspring, it is in the female's interest to be as discriminating as possible.

Selection for indicators

An indicator is any perceivable bodily or behavioural characteristic (e.g. height, facial features) that signals an individual's quality as a mate, revealing information about age, health, strength, etc. These indicators reveal characteristics that might be passed on to offspring (selection for 'good genes') and the likelihood that the mate will provide for, protect and support any offspring (selection for 'good parents'). Zahavi (1991) claims that these indicators must be costly to produce in order to be reliable (the so-called 'handicap principle'); otherwise, they could be faked by low-quality mates.

Selection for provisioning

Provisioning refers to the ability to offer potential mates valuable resources such as food and shelter. By choosing a male who is generous and offers gifts, females are more likely to gain a mate who will share his resources with his family and provide for his partner and any subsequent offspring.

For females, reproduction involves the greater burden of producing eggs, pregnancy and feeding the young; therefore, male provisioning is attractive, as it increases the female's resources and eases their burden (in terms of energy expenditure). The attractiveness of this trait is demonstrated in modern-day **polygynous** hunter-gatherer societies, where the best hunters (i.e. those most successful at provisioning) have the most wives and are also more likely to have extra-marital affairs (Hill and Kaplan 1988).

Facial preferences

The human face plays an important role when choosing a mate, as human facial attractiveness advertises 'good genes'. Individuals with attractive facial features are preferred as mates because of the potential benefits of passing on these attractive characteristics to offspring.

- *Female facial preferences* – According to research (e.g. Thornhill and Gangestad 1999), there are distinct 'masculine' facial characteristics that females find attractive, e.g. large jaw, prominent cheekbones. These characteristics arise as a result of male sex hormones such as testosterone. Because testosterone also suppresses the immune system, only 'healthy' individuals can afford to produce these masculine traits and so are more likely to be selected as mates.

- *Male facial preferences* – Among males, facial preferences are rather different, as they tend to prefer females with child-like features (the 'baby-face hypothesis'). These characteristics indicate youth and fertility, making them more attractive as potential mates (Thornhill and Gangestad 1993).

Short-term mating preferences

Human beings have evolved a number of different mating strategies, some used for short-term (i.e. casual) rather than long-term mating. According to sexual selection, males achieve the greatest reproductive success by impregnating as many females as possible. For females, however, engaging in casual sex can have more serious consequences:

- reputational damage and reduced value as a potential future mate
- lower-quality offspring as a result of mating with a poor-quality male.

For this reason, we would expect significant sex differences in males' and females' motivation for casual sex. This is what Clark and Hatfield (1989) discovered in their study of male and female undergraduates. When approached by an attractive opposite-sex stranger and asked for sex, 75 per cent of males accepted the offer whereas no females did so, thus showing that males, more than females, have evolved a motivation for casual sex.

This topic continues on the next spread. ☞

Essential notes

There is a logic behind sexual selection that makes sex differences entirely predictable. Low-quality mates produce low-quality offspring. Mating with a high-quality partner, on the other hand, produces high-quality offspring and a greater chance of an individual's genes being passed on beyond the next generation.

Examiners' notes

You should always be flexible about how you represent AO1 descriptive material in an answer. There are approximately 800 words of descriptive content on pp. 28–9; an essay question would allow you to use 250 words at most. Therefore, you should be able to précis the points made on these two pages and be prepared to sacrifice some of these in order to add depth to others.

Essential notes

Buss's research demonstrates that sex differences in mate preferences are universal, i.e. common to all cultures. This suggests that human mate preferences are shaped by evolutionary, rather than cultural, factors.

Evaluation of sexual selection and human reproductive behaviour

Research evidence for sex differences in mate preferences

In a study of 37 cultures, Buss (1989) provided evidence to support the claim that there would be universal sex differences in the mate preferences of males and females. For example, Buss found the following:

- Men universally placed more emphasis on physical attractiveness – an indication of a female's health and hence fertility and reproductive value.

- Men of all the cultures studied desired a partner who was younger than they were, an indication that men universally value fertility in potential mates.

- Women, on the other hand, showed a universal preference for men with resources or with characteristics (such as ambition or intelligence) that would translate into resources in the future.

Methodological limitations with the Buss study

The Buss study was a large-scale study spanning several continents, with different sampling methods being used in different countries. This raises questions as to whether it achieved representative sampling across the target populations being studied. For example, rural and less well-educated individuals were underrepresented in the study.

Preferences do not equal real-life choices

Another question arises in the limitations of research that focuses on preferences rather than on real-life choices. For example, people may express a preference for an ideal partner (e.g. attractive, intelligent, ambitious), while accepting that they may have to compromise when it comes to a real-life partner. However, a study of real-life marriages (Buss 1989) has confirmed many of the predictions of sexual selection theory. For example, Buss found that men do choose younger women; furthermore, when they divorce and remarry, they tend to marry women who are increasingly younger than they are.

Support for evolutionary influences on face preferences

- *Early emergence of face preferences* – Humans show differential interest in attractive female faces as early as the first year of infancy, implying that preference for attractive faces is more likely to be an evolved response than a learned behaviour.

- *Cross-cultural agreement* – There is also a significant degree of cross-cultural agreement in ratings of facial attractiveness. For example, infant preference for attractive faces has been observed for a range of human faces, including Caucasian and African-American adult female faces, adult male faces, and infant faces (Kendell-Scott and Stark 2003).

Examiners' notes

Although the AO3 content of essays (which is about research methods) is credited under the more general AO2/AO3 mark allocations (see p. 45), it is a useful way of expanding your critical commentary in an answer. Look closely at the type of method used in a research study:

- What do you know about the strengths and limitations of that particular method of investigation?
- Do any of these strengths or limitations apply here?
- How can you make them *explicitly* relevant?

Female mate preference is linked to their menstrual cycle

Penton-Voak *et al.* (1999) investigated whether women's preference for 'attractive' male faces varied according to the stage of their menstrual cycle. They found the following:

- During their less fertile stages, women seemed to prefer men with softer, more feminine features. This may indicate that a less masculine-looking male makes a better long-term partner, being seen as kinder and more caring – characteristics normally associated with females.
- During the most fertile time of their menstrual cycle, however, women seemed to be attracted to more masculine-looking men, suggesting there might be benefits to be had from short-term mating with more masculine males in order to produce children with 'good genes'.

Evolutionary psychology is not the answer to everything

Nicolson (1999) argues that the relevance of evolutionary factors has been overemphasized and that, in the modern social context, this is not how people *really* live and choose partners – there is a whole range of complex factors influencing human reproductive behaviour.

For example, the claim that human behaviour is constrained by adaptations that developed in our distant ancestors makes sense only if the environmental challenges remain stable over evolutionary time. However, if the environment, including the social environment, is constantly changing (which evidence suggests), then the only kind of mind that makes humans adaptive is one that is flexible and responsive. In some environments, it might be adaptive for males and females to act in the way suggested by sexual selection theory, but not in all. This challenges the claim of these being universal human behaviours.

Issues, debates and approaches (IDA)

Cultural bias in explanations of mate preference

Evolutionary explanations of mate preference quote a waist-to-hip ratio of 0.7 in females as being the ideal indicator of fertility and hence an important characteristic of mate choice. However, studies have shown that in isolated populations in Tanzania and Cameroon (Dixson 2007), men consider such 'hourglass women' as sickly looking. They prefer a waist-to-hip ratio of between 0.8 and 0.9.

Gender bias in explanations of short-term mating

According to the evolutionary explanation of reproductive behaviour, males are more predisposed towards short-term mating than are females. Reproductive success for males is determined solely by the number of fertilizations they can achieve. Females, on the other hand, are less predisposed toward casual sex because the costs of inappropriate matings are much higher. However, Greiling and Buss (2000) suggest that this ignores the possible benefits of short-term mating to the female, including using it to exit a poor-quality relationship or as a way of producing more genetically diverse offspring.

Essential notes

While the findings of the Penten-Voak *et al.* study may seem surprising, we should remember that such preferences among ancestral females would have been adaptive, helping to ensure both the survival and the reproductive success of their children. Modern females, however, may well base their choice of mate on quite different factors.

Examiners' notes

Evolutionary explanations do tend to attract criticisms that lack substance, i.e. are more assertive or speculative than psychologically informed. The criticism given here is developed and offers a logical reason why evolutionary explanations may be limited. If you do criticize the evolutionary perspective, you should make sure that you offer some similar logic (or evidence) to support the claims you are making.

Sex differences in parental investment

Parental investment theory

The idea of 'parental investment' was suggested by Trivers (1972), who defined it as being 'the investment a parent makes in an individual offspring that increases that individual's chances of surviving at the cost of the parent's ability to invest in other offspring'.

In most species, the investment made by males and females is far from equal:

- The female's **gamete** (eggs) are far fewer in number and more costly to produce than the male's gametes (sperm).
- A woman can produce only a limited number of offspring, whereas a man can potentially father an unlimited number.
- The female carries the developing embryo inside her, whereas the male can simply walk away having achieved the task of fertilization.

Men's minimum obligatory investment is, therefore, considerably less than women's. This discrepancy has consequences for the reproductive strategies used by males and females, i.e. there is a pronounced difference between the sexes in terms of mating strategies used (e.g. whether oriented towards short-term or long-term mating). Indiscriminate mating could cost a woman substantial time and resources if conception occurs, whereas indiscriminate reproductive success can be much less costly for a man (Goetz and Shackelford 2009).

Maternal investment

- *Infant dependence on the mother* – The reasons why females invest so heavily prior to childbirth are clear (internal fertilization), but the reasons why females invest so heavily after childbirth are less obvious. One factor is the gradual increase in brain size over the last two million years, which has resulted in a more difficult childbirth (because of the enlargement of the skull). To compensate for this difficulty, childbirth occurs earlier in development than is ideal, and so humans are born relatively immature compared to other animals. As a result, humans are dependent on their parents until at least the teenage years. Human mothers must carry their unborn child for nine months and, after birth, the infants of early humans would have been dependent on their mother's milk for up to two years.

- *Certainty of maternity* – The greater parental investment of females could also be explained because, unlike males, they can be certain that they are the true parent of their child.

Paternal investment

- *Focus on courtship and copulation* – Human males are able to opt out of parental investment in a way that females cannot. By focusing more of their reproductive effort on courtship and copulation, they can afford to devote relatively little of their time to parental care (Daly and Wilson 1978).

Examiners' notes

In exams from 2012 onwards, questions may be asked specifically about sex differences in parental investment – see for example, question 3(b) on p. 58. In exams prior to that, the questions on this topic will be phrased in more general terms, asking about 'evolutionary explanations of parental investment'. You can use the material on pp. 32–5 on sex differences to construct your answer to either type of question.

Essential notes

Parental investment theory states that the sex that makes the larger obligatory parental investment will be the more sexually discriminating, whereas the sex that makes the smaller obligatory parental investment will compete more intensely for access to the higher-investing sex. In humans, this means that females will be the more sexually discriminating, and males will compete for access to the more heavily investing females.

- *Danger of cuckoldry* – Males can never be completely certain that any offspring produced by a female is theirs; they therefore run the risk of using up valuable resources looking after another man's offspring (**cuckoldry**).

- *Shift from mating to parenting* – Given that some level of paternal investment is found in most human societies, it is almost certain that, at some point in our evolutionary past, men benefited by shifting some portion of reproductive effort from mating to parenting (Lovejoy 1981).

Sexual and emotional jealousy

The possibility of sexual infidelity posed different adaptive problems for males and females:

- For a man, an unfaithful mate meant the risk of investing in offspring that were not his own.
- For a woman, an unfaithful mate may have led to the diversion of resources away from her and her offspring.

According to Buss (1995), sexual jealousy may have evolved as a way of responding to these problems, with the different sexes being concerned about different types of infidelity:

- Men are more jealous of sexual infidelity because of the risk of cuckoldry.
- Women are more concerned about emotional infidelity, because if the male shifts emotional attention towards another woman, he might then divert his resources toward her and any offspring from that liaison.

Research on sex differences in parental investment

Parental investment theory suggests that females are better prepared (both physically and psychologically) than males for dealing with parenting.

To demonstrate that these differences are the product of evolution, Geher *et al.* (2007) asked undergraduates (who were not parents) to complete a scale that measured how prepared they perceived themselves to be for parenting.

- The scale found no difference in the perceptions of males and females in their perceived readiness for parenting.

- However, when presented with scenarios that emphasized the *psychological* costs of parenting, males showed significantly higher **autonomic nervous** system arousal.

Summary of sex differences in parental investment

Table 2 summarizes the differences between males and females in terms of parental investment.

This topic continues on the next spread. ☞

Males
• Can produce more offspring
• Have a lower level of parental investment
• May not be sure about paternity
• Place emphasis on multiple mates
Females
• Can produce fewer offspring
• Have a higher level of parental investment
• Can prove child is theirs
• Place emphasis on a single, high-quality mate

Table 2
Summary of sex differences in parental investment

Evaluation of sex differences in parental investment

Consequences of maternal investment: cuckoldry

Infant dependency means that females are attracted to males who provide resources, but females also want to ensure that they have high-quality offspring. One way to achieve this is to marry a man who can provide good resources but to 'shop around' for extra-marital mating opportunities with high-quality males (i.e. men with good genes but few resources). The implication of this claim is that some women may attempt to cuckold their partners.

- *Benefits to women of cuckoldry* – The benefits women would gain from such behaviour would include additional social support from the other male and perhaps higher-quality genes for her children (Geary *et al.* 2004).

- *Risks to women of cuckoldry* – There are risks associated with extra-marital mating, including the possibility of abandonment and the use of **mate-retention strategies** by their current partner (Daly and Wilson 1988), such as threats or violence against the female partner (or against rival males) or the use of emotional manipulation (e.g. threatening to kill themselves).

- *Research support for use of extra-marital affairs* – Bellis and Baker (1990) provide some support for the hypothesis that women use extra-marital mating to obtain 'good genes', showing that when women initiated an infidelity, it often occurred around the time of ovulation. They found that 7 per cent of the copulations around this time were with a male other than their current partner and these copulations were less likely to involve use of contraceptives than copulations with their partner.

Fathers do help out

Research supports the claim that human males do contribute to parenting, and that this is associated with a decrease in infant and child mortality levels, as well as an improvement in the physical health of children. Resources provided by fathers allow the family to live in healthier environments and provide a more stable food supply (Reid 1997).

Cuckoldry is not an issue

Parental investment theory suggests that investment by fathers is greater if they know the child is biologically theirs. They do not want to spend time and resources helping bring up another man's child.

There are, however, studies that contradict this assumption. Anderson (1999) examined the help given by fathers and stepfathers to children and how their relationship with the child's mother affected investment levels. Anderson measured paternal investment in terms of financial support and time spent with the child. The surprising finding was that the men did not discriminate between children born to their current partner from her previous relationship (i.e. stepchildren) and their own child from a previous relationship (i.e. their biological offspring).

Essential notes

As a reproductive strategy, cuckoldry may be adaptive for women, as a way of benefiting from one man's good genes and another man's resources. However, it's a strategy that comes with risks.

Examiners' notes

One way of elaborating your AO2 is to attempt to *explain* surprising findings such as the Anderson study described here. A possible reason for this finding is that a man may invest less in children from a previous failed relationship because he cannot be sure the children are his own. However, by investing in the children of his current partner, he may be able to convince her that he is a 'good provider' and so promote future mating opportunities. This contradicts the idea that biological similarity is essential and suggests that parental investment is a more complex issue than suggested by this theory.

Evidence for sex differences in jealousy

- Buss *et al.* (1992) provides support for the claim that males are more likely to experience sexual jealousy and females more likely to experience emotional jealousy. Male students showed a higher galvanic skin response (GSR) – an objective measure of emotional arousal – when asked to imagine sexual infidelity by their partner, whereas female students showed greater GSR arousal when presented with concerns about emotional infidelity.

- Harris (2003), however, found that men respond with greater arousal to any sexual imagery, regardless of its context, and therefore questions whether such sex differences are an adaptive response. She suggests that sex differences in jealousy are more likely to be a product of social learning than of evolutionary history.

Methodological issues with supporting research

The Geher *et al.* study measured both how ready men and women felt about becoming parents and their level of arousal, which was felt to be an indication of how ready they actually were. However, differences in perceived parental readiness would be affected by the **social desirability bias**, in that participants may have given the answers they felt were appropriate (i.e. males stating that they were more ready than they actually were). Males may well recognize the importance of *appearing* to have parental potential and so are more likely to be motivated to see themselves as being capable of parenting.

Issues, debates and approaches (IDA)

Alternative perspectives on paternal investment

An evolutionary perspective is limited when explaining the possibility of paternal investment. According to Rowe (2002), men's parenting depends instead on various personal and social conditions, including:
- inherited individual differences in parenting emphasis
- personality characteristics
- the quality of the relationship with the mother
- the characteristics of the child.

Research also suggests that childhood experiences such as parental divorce are correlated with the degree to which men invest in the upbringing and care of their children (Belsky *et al.* 1991).

Insights from non-human species

Explanations of the evolution of human parental behaviour can be informed by making a comparative analysis of parental investment in species related in evolutionary terms. The two species most closely related to humans are chimpanzees and bonobos. However, in both these species, males show little or no paternal investment. Therefore, the emergence of the current human pattern of parental behaviour (e.g. an increase in male parenting) would require either dramatic evolutionary changes from our primate ancestors or the contribution of cultural learning.

Essential notes

As the name suggests, GSR devices work by analysing the skin, picking up autonomic responses such as sweat. Readings can be used as a measure of anxiety, stress or general emotional arousal. GSR, therefore, uses the body's automatic responses to measure how a person is feeling rather than the researcher relying solely on what the person tells them (which may be subject to social desirability bias – see below).

Examiners' notes

All questions on the A2 Unit 3 examination require *some* IDA content. However, it is not sufficient just to tag random IDA material at the end of an answer. Examiners are looking for this information to be woven effectively into your essay and for it to form a substantive part of your evaluation. See pp. 46–7 for more advice on including IDA in your answers.

The influence of childhood on adult relationships

Parent–child relationships

The internal working model

Bowlby (1982) suggested that a child's primary attachment figure was the 'blueprint' for subsequent relationships in their life. Based on their childhood experiences with their primary attachment figure, the individual forms a schema of:

- what a relationship is
- how reliable and available the attachment figure is
- the sorts of emotional experience they might expect.

These **internal working models** influence the child's expectations about future relationships. Adult relationships are therefore also likely to reflect early **attachment styles** (i.e. whether secure or insecure).

Attachment and adult relationships

A study by Hazan and Shaver (1987) investigated the link between attachment style and later adult relationships. They used a questionnaire (the 'love quiz'), which asked adults to comment on their early attachment experiences and the most important romantic relationship of their life so far. They found the following:

- People who were securely attached as infants tended to have happy and lasting relationships in adulthood. They also believed that love was both enduring and based on mutual trust.
- Adults who had been insecurely attached as infants found adult relationships more difficult and were more likely to be divorced; they were also more pessimistic about the possibility of finding 'true love'.

This study therefore provides evidence for Bowlby's idea of the internal working model and his claim that early experiences influence later relationships.

Simpson *et al.* (2007) provide further support for the importance of early attachment experiences for shaping adult relationships. They studied 78 participants at four key points in their life. The researchers found that participants who were securely attached as infants:

- were rated as having higher levels of social competence as children
- were closer to their friends as 16 year olds
- were more expressive and more emotionally attached to their romantic partners in early adulthood.

Attachment style and marital satisfaction

Feeney (1996) examined the relationship between attachment style and marital satisfaction. She believed there would be a relationship between attachment style and caregiving, and that this, in turn, would affect how satisfied someone was in their relationship. Feeney found that secure attachment was associated with supportive caregiving to the partner and that marital satisfaction was higher for securely attached individuals.

Feeney (1999) further examined the relationship between attachment style and emotional experience in adult relationships. She found that insecure attachment was associated with less frequent and intense positive emotions, and with more frequent and intense negative emotions toward the spouse. These results suggest that attachment plays a role in influencing the emotional climate of a marriage, which, in turn, influences marital satisfaction.

Interaction with peers

Interaction with peers in childhood

Research has also investigated the importance of children's interactions with their peers as an influence on their relationships in adulthood:

- Qualter and Munn (2005) found that children's interactions with other children enable them to learn more about themselves; they internalize these experiences and develop expectations about future relationships. For example, their interactions with other children give them a sense of their own value (e.g. their popularity, their ability to satisfy others and so on). These internalized expectations influence how they approach adult relationships in much the same way as the internal working model outlined earlier.
- Nangle *et al.* (2003) highlight the importance of friendship in this process. Having a close friend to trust and confide in helps children learn how to take part in emotionally intimate relationships, through feelings of acceptance and of being understood by another person. These characteristics are important in later romantic relationships.

Interaction with peers in adolescence

During adolescence, individuals are faced with the important 'psychological tasks' of preparing for adulthood, which involves establishing autonomy, independence and more intimate relationships. Friendships, which were important during childhood, therefore assume an even greater significance and depth during adolescence. For example, Frey and Rothlisberger (1996) found that adolescents had twice as many relationships with peers than with family. Blos (1967) suggested that relationships with peers help the adolescent avoid feelings of loneliness, without having to make any commitment to a long-term partner; they provide a 'way-station' on the route to achieving separation from parents and 'individuation'. Erikson (1968) believed that peers are important for healthy identity development because they allow adolescents to:

- explore different identities
- let go of their psychological dependence on parents
- try out their skills at forming intimate relationships with others.

According to Kirchler *et al.* (1993), those adolescents who remain closely attached to their families and do not develop peer relationships may have difficulty in establishing their autonomy and engaging in adult relationships.

This topic continues on the next spread. ☞

Essential notes

Research suggests that early relationships with peers are also important in shaping young people's attitudes to adult relationships, with peer relationships assuming a more significant role during adolescence.

Examiners' notes

Many A2 questions are divided into parts – (a), (b), etc. – which means you could be asked to provide elements of this material in different forms. Each question has a maximum of 8 marks out of 24 for AO1 description (9 marks out of 25 prior to 2012). Therefore, in a straightforward essay such as 'Discuss the effects of early experiences on adult relationships' for 24 marks (25 prior to 2012), you should write 200 to 240 words of AO1 description that should be a balance of breadth and depth. A good approach would be to choose four or five of the points on these two pages and précis each to about 40–50 words.

Alternatively, reference to this area may form part of a question, e.g. 'Outline the effects of early experiences on adult relationships' for 4 or 5 marks. This would require between 100 and 120 words, so could either be two points at 50–60 words each or, perhaps more effectively, three points at 35–40 words for each point.

Evaluation of childhood influences on adult relationships

Research evidence for the association between attachment and adult relationships

The association between attachment style and adult relationships is supported by Morrison *et al.* (1997), who asked college students in the United States to complete questionnaires describing their current or most recent intimate relationship and an attachment style inventory to assess their attachment style.

- Students with secure attachment styles described more interdependence in their relationships.
- Students with avoidant or ambivalent attachment styles described more hostility in their intimate relationships than did students with a secure style.

Fraley (1998) carried out a meta-analysis of studies in this area and found significant positive correlations for the relationship between early attachment style and quality of later adult relationships.

Methodological issues with the Simpson *et al.* study

The longitudinal approach used by Simpson *et al.* (2007) in their research, described on p. 36, was particularly appropriate, because it enabled the researchers to find out whether the attachment experiences of individual children influenced later romantic relationships. This type of study cannot determine causality, but it does enable researchers to predict likely outcomes in specified circumstances with a fair degree of confidence. In this case, children with more secure attachment experiences appeared to enjoy better-quality romantic relationships in adulthood.

Problems with retrospective data in research

For many of the studies in this area, there is a reliance on retrospective data – that is, participants must recall experiences from their childhood, with the data then being correlated with variables, such as marital satisfaction in adulthood. In the Hazan and Shaver study on p. 36, for example, participants were asked to remember their childhood experiences. Given that some of the participants were in their 80s, their memory of childhood experience was unlikely to be completely accurate, which creates problems for the validity of the data obtained and any conclusions drawn from this data.

Social desirability bias

Researchers in this field must frequently make use of self-report measures, and this has its problems, particularly in a sensitive area such as relationships. Participants may want to give a good impression of how well adjusted and secure they are in their relationships. This means there is the possibility that there was a social desirability effect on participants' responses, and the reliability of the data may have been weakened.

The negative side of adolescent relationships

Research appears to show that adolescent relationships are an important influence on later adult relationships, but there appear to be some more negative aspects to adolescent relationships:

Examiners' notes

Be careful about speculating about what might be the case in a particular study. For example, when using the social desirability bias as a way of evaluating the methodology of survey research, you may find that researchers actually took steps to stop this being a problem. For example, in the Hazan and Shaver study (see p. 36), participants sent their responses in anonymously, which mean they were less likely to have been subject to the social desirability bias. This in itself is a positive critical point that you can make because it adds to the validity of the findings.

- *Association with deviant behaviour* – Haynie (2003) found a significant association between romantic involvement and **deviant behaviour**, with increases in deviant behaviour rising to as much as 35 per cent among those adolescents who were regularly involved in romantic relationships.

- *Lower academic achievement and greater behavioural problems* – According to Neeman *et al.* (1995), romantic involvement in early and middle adolescence was found to be associated with a decrease in academic achievement and an increase in behaviour problems. By later adolescence, however, this was no longer the case.

Attachment disorders

Some children who fail to bond with a caregiver in infancy may become unable to form healthy social relationships as adults, developing what is called **reactive attachment disorder** (RAD). This is a severe disorder characterized by the non-development of the child's social abilities. It can present itself in different forms:

- inhibited form – a lack of responsiveness towards, and a complete mistrust of, almost everyone
- disinhibited form – an inability to discriminate in relationships, treating strangers with excessive familiarity or treating everybody as if they were their best friend.

RAD can be caused by a number of factors, including child neglect, abuse, abrupt separation from caregivers or frequent changes in caregivers (such as in children's homes).

Issues, debates and approaches (IDA)

Determinism in research

Many of the studies on these pages appear to indicate that early experiences (such as early attachment style) have a fixed influence on later adult relationships. For example, there is the implication that children who are insecurely attached in childhood will experience emotionally unsatisfying relationships as adults. However, this is not the case, as researchers such as Simpson and colleagues also found many examples of adults who were experiencing happy and satisfying adult relationships despite having been insecurely attached as children.

Cultural differences

Parenting style varies cross-culturally (Martin and Colbert 1997); it therefore stands to reason that the influence of childhood experience on adult relationships will also vary cross-culturally.

Research (Takahashi 1990; Hanano 1999) has also found cross-cultural differences in both infant attachment style and adult attachment style. As a result, it is likely that the internal working model of children in different cultures will differ, as will its influence on adult relationships in those cultures.

The influence of culture on romantic relationships

Individualism and collectivism

Most Western cultures are individualistic, placing emphasis on the individual person and their rights, goals, aspirations and so on. Individual performance and achievement are praised, while reliance on others may be regarded as undesirable or a weakness. Hofstede's anthropological research (Hofstede 1980) allowed him to place each culture studied along a continuum from collectivist to individualist (see Fig. 4).

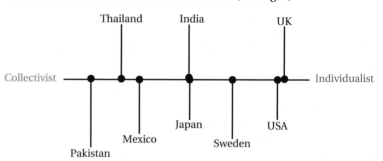

Fig. 4
A continuum of cultures from collectivist to individualist

- In **individualist cultures**, such as the UK and the USA, there is greater emphasis on 'I' rather than 'we' in interpersonal relationships. Where there is a conflict between the goals of the individual and the goals of the collective (e.g. group or society), personal needs are considered more important.

- In **collectivist cultures**, such as Pakistan or Thailand, more value is placed on the 'we' than the 'I'. The desires of particular individuals are considered less important than ties between, and responsibilities to, collective units (such as family or community). In their social relationships, members of collectivist cultures are encouraged to be *interdependent* rather than autonomous, and marriage is often seen more as a union between *families* than a union between individuals (Moghaddam *et al.* 1993).

Relationships in different cultures

Various factors affect how relationships are formed, including the geographical and social mobility, and degree of choice.

Geographical and social mobility, and partner choice

- In many Western, industrialized societies, people enjoy considerable geographical and social mobility. They are free to interact with a relatively large number of people on a daily basis. When it comes to the formation of relationships, there is a greater choice of potential partners and fewer restrictions on choice.

- More traditional, non-Western cultures offer less geographical and social mobility and so individuals have less choice in whom they interact with. The available 'pool' of potential, suitable romantic partners is, therefore, considerably smaller.

Voluntary or arranged?

- In Western, individualist societies, people generally expect to be able to choose their own partner, and the primary basis for marriage is expected to be romantic love. Parental consent is considered desirable, but by no means necessary.

- In countries with a collectivist orientation, the criteria for selecting individuals to be joined as a couple include family alliances, economic arrangements between families and health. The traditional system of mate selection is characterized by a marriage that is *arranged* by families of the two individuals.

Cultural differences in romantic love

The universality of romantic love

Given the differences outlined above, it would be logical to conclude that romantic love would be common only in Western, industrialized cultures and would be less important in traditional, more collectivist cultures. However, this appears not to be the case. Jankowiak and Fisher (1992) investigated 166 hunting and gathering societies and found clear evidence of passionate, romantic love in most of the societies they studied. In only one society was there no compelling evidence of romantic love.

The importance of love in marital relationships

- Sprecher *et al.* (1994) wanted to find out whether people from different cultures would marry somebody that had all the qualities they desired, but whom they did not love. They asked 1 667 students from America, Japan and Russia. The Japanese (81 per cent) and Americans (89 per cent) expressed a very high reluctance to marry in the absence of love. The Russian students were more practical about marriage, and the women in particular (59 per cent) were more likely to settle for a loveless marriage.

- Levine *et al.* (1995) carried out a similar study, investigating love as a basis for marriage in 11 countries. Again, the US respondents recorded the highest figure when asked whether they would refuse to marry someone they did not love (86 per cent), whereas the figures for students from traditional, collectivist cultures such as India (24 per cent) and Thailand (34 per cent) suggest a much greater proportion were prepared to marry someone they did not love. In such societies, the extended family continues to be of primary importance, and romantic love is considered a luxury.

Cultural differences in online relationships

In 'real-life', face-to-face interactions, people typically start by exchanging non-intimate details about themselves early on, gradually opening up and

This topic continues on the next spread. ☞

Essential notes

Jankowiak and Fischer concluded that romantic attraction is a distinct emotional motivational system present in all human beings. All human beings, regardless of cultural background, appear to crave romantic love. This suggests that love serves some universal adaptive function for human beings, which explains why it is so widespread.

sharing more intimate information as they begin to trust their partner. Ma (1996) studied Internet relationships to find out whether people more readily break these rules of self-disclosure when online. Ma found that both East Asian and North American college students tended towards more rapid self-disclosure in Internet, compared with face-to-face, interactions. However, in relationships between American and East Asian students, the American students perceived *themselves* to be more self-disclosing.

Evaluation of research into Western and non-Western relationships

Individualism versus collectivism

Much of the research into cultural differences in relationships has used Hofstede's (1980) original distinction between individualist and collectivist cultures as an underpinning assumption. However, questions have been raised as to how useful this distinction actually is, particularly with the results of more recent research. In a study of people's attitudes towards various types of relationship, Li *et al.* (2006) found very few differences in the attitudes of people from Canada (an individualist culture) and China (a collectivist culture), but it *did* show differences between the Chinese and Indian samples (both collectivist cultures).

The changing face of 'arranged' marriages

Some researchers have investigated what has happened when families from collectivist cultures migrate to settle in countries whose predominant ethos is individualistic. Many Asian communities living in the UK seem to be moving gradually from the traditional patterns of mate selection (including arranged marriages) towards a more Westernized approach of letting individuals choose their own partner, although still with parental consent. Research (e.g. Goodwin *et al.* 1997) suggests that many Asian immigrant families have undergone substantial changes in their attitude to marriage and romantic relationships, compared with families in their country of origin.

Choice may not be linked to satisfaction

Worldwide, arranged marriages are a widespread occurrence, but few studies have compared levels of satisfaction in arranged marriages compared to marriages of choice. One study that has done so is by Myers *et al.* (2005), who compared the levels of satisfaction of individuals living in arranged marriages in India with those of individuals living in marriages of choice in the USA. Respondents were asked to complete a questionnaire measuring marital satisfaction, as well as the characteristics they considered to be important in a marriage.

- The most significant finding of this study was that there were no differences in marital satisfaction between people living in arranged marriages and marriages of choice.

- Some cultural differences were found, however, with regard to the factors considered important for a successful marriage. For example, those living in the US placed a high priority on love as a precursor to marriage, whereas in India, love was regarded as less important.

These results suggest that, regardless of the different factors considered important in the two cultures, satisfaction with one's marital relationship is not affected.

The consequences of increasing urbanization on divorce

Impermanence has become a feature of relationships in the West, although it is a relatively recent phenomenon. Fifty years ago, divorce was relatively rare but, with greater urbanization and mobility, the shift to more non-permanent relationships in the West has become marked.

Researchers have investigated whether there is similar shift in different types of culture around the world. For example, India has shown a sharp increase in divorce rates in recent years, with most of those splitting up being members of India's thriving, urban middle class (Dummett 2011).

Research findings suggest that the relationship differences found in a range of cultures may not be a product of Western versus non-Western differences – or even individualist versus collectivist features – but rather may be a product of increasing urbanization in societies around the world.

Issues, debates and approaches (IDA)

An evolutionary perspective on romantic love

Offering an evolutionary perspective on the value of romantic love, Pinker (2008) suggests that love is a species-specific adaptation that has evolved to promote survival and reproduction among human beings. Since research has found that being in a long-term committed relationship is associated with lower mortality rates, increased happiness and decreased levels of stress, this would appear to support Pinker's claim that there is a clear adaptive value to being in a long-term relationship.

If love does indeed have adaptive value, we would expect to find its existence in all human societies, regardless of whether they are traditional or industrialized. Jankowiak and Fischer's (1992) study of traditional societies (see p. 41) found that was indeed the case. So, what we now call 'romantic love' would have helped to keep our distant ancestors alive long enough to reproduce and pass on their genes.

Cultural bias in relationship research

Any aspect of methodology that behaves in a specified way in one culture, and one culture only, creates a cultural bias that may invalidate any conclusions from a cross-cultural study. Measures of 'love' and 'satisfaction' developed in Western cultures, for example, may not be valid in other cultures. Such cultural bias in research takes no account of what is important in that 'other' culture.

Kim and Berry (1993) have suggested that we should aim to develop *indigenous* psychologies, whereby we study factors that have developed within particular cultures and are seen as important and *meaningful* within those cultures.

Essential notes

Divorce rates may not be a good source of data for making a judgment on marital satisfaction. This is because someone may not be happy in a marriage, but feels obliged to stay in it for various reasons. The occurrence of a divorce may indicate *dissatisfaction*, but the absence of one does not necessarily indicate *satisfaction*.

Examiners' notes

In order to qualify as IDA material, you should try to move beyond just *describing* cultural or gender differences. Instead, consider how any such differences might constitute a cultural or gender bias in research. For example, the fact that there are cultural differences in the meaning of love might create problems in studies that use Western measures of love to investigate cultural differences in how important love is in non-Western cultures.

Answering A2 examination questions

AO1, AO2 and AO3

The A2 examination assesses three 'assessment objectives' known as AO1, AO2 and AO3:

- AO1 assesses your ability to recall and show your understanding of scientific knowledge – e.g. describing a theory or study.
- AO2 assesses your ability to analyse and evaluate scientific knowledge – e.g. evaluating a theory in terms of research support.
- AO3 is concerned with 'How Science Works' – e.g. methodological criticisms of research studies.

Examiners' notes

On this Unit 3 paper, AO1 is worth 9 marks (8 marks from 2012) of every question, and AO2/AO3 is worth 16 marks of every question. This is very important, as it should inform the way you structure your response to exam questions.

Be prepared

A2 questions will often occur as questions in parts and these different parts can also occur with different mark allocations. For example, question (a) on a particular topic could be worth:

- 4, 5 or 9 marks (for exams up to 2011), or
- 4 or 8 marks (for exams from 2012 onwards).

This means that not only should you be aware of all the topics on which you may be questioned, but you should also have practised examination type answers for these to fit the varying mark allocations.

For example, if you have covered the Unit 3 topic of relationships and included the sociobiological explanation as one of your theories of relationship formation, then you should be able to produce a 'shorter version' outline of the theory to answer a shorter 4- or 5-mark question, as well as being able to produce a 'longer version' outline of the explanation for an 8- or 9-mark question. This has two clear benefits:

- You will have the information you need to produce enough descriptive material for a higher mark allocation question.
- You won't waste valuable exam time by overproducing an answer for a smaller mark allocation.

Examiners' notes

At AS level, there are distinct questions (and mark allocations) for AO3, but at A2 level this is not the case, and AO3 is simply part of your AO2 mark allocation (referred to as AO2/AO3). This is justified because in evaluating theories and/or research studies, you will invariably include some of the research evidence, ethical issues, reliability, validity, etc., that constitute AO3.

Use your time wisely

Examinations are held under time constraints, and so you must use your time wisely. Students often waste far too much time doing things that are not required, e.g. stating *'In this essay I am going to…'* or providing irrelevant information. This means that they don't have sufficient time to do the things they should be doing, and so lose many of the marks available.

Read for understanding

When reading a question, ensure that you fully understand its requirements. Far too often, students focus in on a certain word or phrase that identifies the particular topic being examined and base their answer solely on that. After expending much time and effort, they then realize that they are not answering the question as it should be answered or discover they cannot answer the question as well as they first imagined. Therefore, make sure you have read the entire question and fully understand its requirements *before* starting to answer it.

Make a plan

When you have fully understood the question and have decided that you are able to answer it, then it's also a good idea to prepare a small plan of points to be made, possibly in bullet point form numbered in a logical order. This not only gives you a plan to follow, but also protects against forgetting some of these points mid-answer. It also helps you to engage with the material, which again is a useful strategy towards producing higher-quality answers.

Effective evaluation

Students can often become confused, especially under exam conditions, as to what to include in an answer requiring evaluation. A good way to combat this problem is to include the 'recipe' method as a regular part of your revision. Thus, when planning the evaluative content for an answer, list all the different elements that could comprise evaluation. This will vary slightly from question to question depending on the wording, but generally you should have:

- examples of research that both supports and weakens points being made
- practical applications
- IDA points (see below)
- methodological points (especially in questions specifically about research studies)
- implications
- theoretical support.

You may not actually use all of this material, but you should produce answers with good breadth of evaluation, as well as reducing the chances of having insufficient material or of using non-creditworthy material.

Issues, debates and approaches (IDA)

An important feature of the AO2 marking allocation is that examiners look for evidence of issues, debates or approaches in your answer. There are many different ways of addressing this requirement, including the following:

- *issues* – gender and cultural bias, ethical issues, real world application
- *debates* – psychology as science, reductionism, free will/ determinism, nature/nurture
- *approaches* – biological, evolutionary, psychodynamic, etc.

Examiners' notes

For the AQA Unit 3 exam paper, you have 90 minutes to answer three questions, i.e. 30 minutes per question. This means that, for each answer, you should spend 10 minutes on your AO1 (description) content and 20 minutes on your AO2 (evaluation) content. This is an essential division, because there are twice as many marks awarded for AO2 as for AO1.

Examiners' notes

As is the case with all AO2 material, IDA should go beyond a couple of brief points tagged on to the end of an answer. It should be appropriate critical commentary woven into your answer and should be elaborated to make it effective.

Opportunities for IDA are flagged up throughout this book, so it is a good idea to practise generating these for all the topics relevant to A2 relationships.

Elaboration in AO2 evaluation

AO2 assesses your ability to analyse and evaluate scientific knowledge relevant to a specific topic area. When allocating marks for AO2 questions, examiners look for appropriateness and *elaboration*. One way of elaborating effectively is to use the 'three-point rule'. This involves:

- *identifying* the critical point
- *justifying* it
- *explaining* why this is good (or bad) for the theory or explanation being evaluated.

For example, if your criticism is that a study lacks ecological validity, this point can be elaborated thus:

> 'This study lacks validity (*identification*), because research by X failed to replicate the findings of Y (*justification*), which therefore means that the findings of Y's research cannot be generalized beyond the specific situation of that experiment (*explanation*)'.

Using the right terminology

As well as having a good understanding of psychological concepts and topics, you also need to be able to communicate your understanding to others. A useful and simple means of achieving this is by using psychological terminology wherever relevant in exam answers. Try to develop a good working knowledge of psychological terminology throughout your studies – and practise using it – in order to become proficient in this skill. However, be careful not to use jargon for its own sake, as this can lead to the danger of writing incomprehensible answers that appear muddled.

Example questions and answers with examiner comments

On the following pages you will find sample questions followed by sample average and strong answers, and also tinted boxes containing the comments and advice of examiners. Answers refer to content within the revision section of this book and additional content, providing you with the opportunity to consolidate and extend your revision and research.

Examiners' notes

It is worth placing obvious 'tags' on your evaluation to make sure the examiner acknowledges it as such. For example, instead of just *describing* a supporting research study, you should preface any such description with a phrase such as 'This claim is supported by research by… which showed that…'.

Examiners' notes

A characteristic of high-grade answers is that they make extensive use of appropriate psychological terminology. Hence, using terms such as 'infidelity' and 'cuckolded' rather than 'sleeping around' and 'being made a mug' demonstrate your familiarity with these concepts and your ability to construct informed responses using the correct terminology.

Example Paper 1

Question 1

Part (a)

Outline the relationship between sexual selection and human reproductive behaviour.
[9 marks (2009 onwards)] **[8 marks** (2012 onwards)]

There are a number of important things to note here.
- This part of the question calls exclusively for descriptive (AO1) material; therefore, any (AO2) evaluation will not gain any marks. Including evaluation would also waste valuable exam time.
- As there is an allocation of 9 marks (8 marks from 2012), a longer, more detailed outline of the relationship is required than if only 4 or 5 marks had been available.

- You could use research studies to highlight features of your answer, but would need to take care to do this in a descriptive rather than an evaluative manner.

Average answer

Sexual selection is all about what makes individuals attractive to members of the opposite sex so that they fancy them as a possible sexual partner. To be attractive in this way means that individuals will have to possess and demonstrate certain qualities, like being pretty for example. These types of qualities form what is known as intrasexual selection. Individuals also need to possess and demonstrate characteristics that allow them to compete with members of their own gender so that they can gain access to members of the opposite sex – for example, males being strong and muscular so that they can be dominant against other males. This is intersexual selection.

These types of qualities help individuals gain access to reproduction opportunities, by which means they can get their genes into the next generation. These characteristics, like female attractiveness, which makes them seem fertile, and male qualities that demonstrate ability to gain and control resources, mainly evolved in the E.E.A. or Pleistocene era. This was around 10,000 to 5 million years ago. During this time, natural selection favoured female and male qualities that helped them to be attractive to members of the opposite sex. These qualities were then passed on to the next generation and so on, until such qualities became more widespread.

This student shows they have an understanding of what sexual selection is, as well as the evolutionary concept of natural selection. They also seem to comprehend that sexual selection is related to human reproductive behaviour in terms of the opportunities for reproduction that it creates. The student also uses psychological terminology to demonstrate their knowledge of the area, e.g. intrasexual and intersexual selection. However, what the student *doesn't* do is communicate this understanding very efficiently or demonstrate a detailed knowledge of the area.

Overall, this is an outline of an answer that never really comes to terms with the question. For instance, this student talks about female attractiveness and its relationship to fertility, but there is no explanation of what female attractiveness consists of and in what ways the quality advertises fertility. In contrast, the 'Strong answer' (see opposite) is much more focused on the question and contains a lot more specific detail.

Examiners see a lot of answers like these – they are not poor answers, but moderate ones that, with practice and focused revision, could easily be turned into good-quality answers.

Strong answer

Humans are sexually dimorphic, males and females possessing different characteristics, like male muscularity. This situation occurred through natural selection, as the evolution of different characteristics brought adaptive advantages to both genders. If a characteristic advanced the chances of being selected as a mate, then it became favoured as a sexually selected one. As sexual reproduction is the only way to further oneself genetically, then being sexually selected as a mate became of paramount importance.

Body symmetry is an indicator of genetic fitness and therefore acts as a universal form of sexual attraction. Individuals with body symmetry are more likely to be selected as sexual partners, with facial symmetry regarded as the best predictor of body symmetry. Individuals with body symmetry report about three times more sexual partners than individuals with asymmetrical bodies. Females especially select males on the basis of body symmetry, as the characteristic requires genetic precision and thus only good genetic quality males can produce it. Any sons produced by couplings with such males should have the same desirable quality themselves, again heightening reproductive ability.

Waist-to-hip ratio is a characteristic indicating the degree of female fertility and thus sexual attractiveness, with a larger waist-to-hip ratio associated with better health status and greater reproductive ability, i.e. 'child-bearing hips'. Indeed, males tend to give more importance overall to physical attractiveness in females due to its indication of fertility. Thus, males look for youthfulness, a vital lustre to hair and skin, which advertises good health, and full breasts to demonstrate excellent child-nurturing ability. Age isn't a good indicator of fertility in males, nor can their fertility be assessed accurately from physical appearance, and anyway female reproductive success is less dependent on finding fertile males, they are looking more for resource-richness.

This is a relevant, accurate and clearly expressed answer that concentrates on a particular area of the topic, i.e. sexual attractiveness. It is well focused throughout on the relationship between sexual attractiveness and human sexual behaviour, with the main focus being on how sexually dimorphic characteristics have evolved in terms of their enhancing opportunities for sexual reproduction.

Both female and male characteristics are covered, with females being described in some breadth and depth concerning qualities of physical attractiveness and males covered similarly in terms of symmetry and resource richness.

This student uses only descriptive material, which the question calls for, even using research evidence concerning the sexual superiority of symmetrical individuals in a descriptive manner.

Part (b)

*Evaluate **one** theory of romantic relationship formation and **one** theory of romantic relationship breakdown.*
[16 marks]

- This part of the question calls exclusively for *evaluative* material, so you must resist the urge to *outline* theories of relationship formation and breakdown, as outlining theories will gain no marks and simply waste valuable exam time.
- There is a clear requirement for only *one* theory of relationship formation and *one* theory of relationship breakdown. If you offered more than one, all would be marked, but only the best one credited. However, you could use other relevant theories as evaluation if they were used as a form of comparison.

- You could use research support to evaluate your chosen theories.
- There is also a need to include pertinent IDA (issues, debates and approaches) comments, e.g. by focusing on strengths and weaknesses of the evolutionary approach (if the sociobiological explanation was used) or by including practical applications (such as in relationship counselling).
- The focus of the question is on evaluating *theories*; evaluation should not, therefore, be centred too much on the *methodology* of studies or else the evaluation becomes more one of research studies than theories.

Average answer

The reinforcement and need satisfaction explanation sees conditioning as explaining how relationships form and, as such, is a behaviourist explanation. Others directly reinforce us through operant conditioning by meeting our psychological needs for things like love and sex, or indirectly reward us because they become associated with pleasant circumstances or outcomes. This was demonstrated by Cunningham (1988) who got males to watch either a happy or sad film and then interact with a female. Those watching the happy film reported more positive interactions, supporting the idea that people form relationships with those they associate with pleasant circumstances. This was backed up by Griffit and Guay (1969), who evaluated participants on a creative task, and if the evaluation was positive, the participants expressed more liking of a non-involved bystander. This suggests we like people who're associated with positive outcomes, so we're more likely to form relationships with them. Overall though, this theory explains friendships more than romantic relationships, because we often make friends with those people we have good times with and who reciprocate our needs, but long-term relationships are much more intricate than this.

Lee (1984) presented a stage model with five stages that explained the break-up of relationships. This theory sees relationship break-ups as being a process that occurs in a logical sequence of stages over a period of time. ☞

The student obviously has a decent working knowledge of the reinforcement and need satisfaction explanation and communicates it reasonably well. Unfortunately, though, time and effort are wasted outlining the explanation, which the question doesn't call for.

The answer only becomes relevant – and starts earning marks – when they use Cunningham's (1998) and Griffit and Guay's (1969) studies to evaluate the explanation. This is done well, with the student showing how the evidence supports the theory; the comment about the theory explaining friendships more than romantic partnerships builds well onto this. There is, however, a noticeable lack of IDA comments in this part of the answer.

These stages are distinct from each other rather than just being a single event. The first stage is dissatisfaction with the relationship, followed by exposure of this dissatisfaction to one's partner. After this the couple negotiate over the nature of the dissatisfaction, then attempts are made to resolve the dissatisfaction and finally, if this dissatisfaction isn't resolved, the relationship ends. The explanation isn't without criticism; Akert (1998) found the partner who instigates a break-up suffers less negative consequences and this therefore suggests there are individual differences in the effects of break-up that the theory doesn't consider. Also, Argyle and Henderson (1984) investigated the role of rule violations in romantic relationship breakdowns, finding them to be important, such as jealousy, lack of tolerance for third-party relationships and public criticism. This implies Lee's explanation isn't a complete one, as it doesn't account for these important features. Lee's explanation is also reductionist, as it only focuses on romantic, heterosexual relationships and therefore can't be applied to friendships or homosexual relationships.

It's a similar story with the second part of this answer. The student wastes valuable time and gains no credit by outlining Lee's model of dissolution (albeit briefly and concisely). The answer only becomes evaluative – and starts gaining marks – with the mention of Akert's (1998) and Argyle and Henderson's (1984) studies. Again, these studies are used quite well, with evidence being focused on shortcomings of the explanation.

The final sentence makes a reasonable IDA point concerning the reductionist nature of the model, but other relevant IDA points could have been embedded seamlessly into the answer to improve its overall quality, e.g. by saying that Duck's model has practical applications in relationship counselling. Such points work even better if they contain detail – e.g. that for a dissatisfied couple who have reached the exposure stage, counsellors could focus on re-establishing affection to save the relationship.

Average answer: overall comment

Looking at the responses to parts (a) and (b) combined, this is a decent enough answer, but too much time is wasted on material that is not creditworthy, with not enough attention given to the more important AO2 material. This would be around the standard of a Grade C answer.

Strong answer

The sociobiological theory of relationship formation offers a plausible explanation for the evolution of mate preferences and has research support. For instance Davis's (1990) content analysis of personal advertisements found males look for health and attractiveness, while offering resources in the form of wealth. Females were looking for resources and status, while advertising beauty and youth, which supports the idea of evolutionary based gender differences in relationship formation. This was backed up by Pawlowski and Dunbar's finding that women aged 35–50 hid their age in personal advertisements, suggesting they do this to attract high-quality partners before reproductive opportunities are ended by the menopause, again in line with the sociobiological ☞

This answer provides an impressive appraisal of the sociobiological explanation that is purely evaluative and contains no description of the theory, which is exactly what the question asks for. The student brings in a number of research studies based on content analysis of personal advertisements, allowing them to build an effective commentary around the degree of support these studies offer to the explanation.

explanation. An everyday example of this is how women will use cosmetics to alter their appearance to seem more youthful and thus fertile.

Further research support comes from Dunbar (1995), who found from personal advertisements that 42% of males sought youthfulness, compared to only 25% of females, while 44% of males sought attractiveness, compared to only 22% of females. This supports the sociobiological notion that males and females are subject to different evolutionary pressures and thus have different reasons for forming relationships. However, the explanation can be said to support gender stereotypes of housebound mothers and sexually promiscuous males, as well as being reductionist, seeing relationships as a means of reproduction, therefore disregarding other reasons for being in romantic relationships, like companionship.

Duck's model of dissolution can be seen to be gender biased, as it doesn't consider several important gender differences. Kassin (1996) reported that women are more likely to want to end relationships due to unhappiness and incompatibility, while males blame a lack of sex for relationships ending. Also women want to remain friends after break-ups, while males generally want a clean break and to start again elsewhere. These findings were backed up by Argyle (1988), who reported that females tend to identify a lack of emotional support as a reason for relationship dissolution, while males reported an absence of fun. Again this suggests Duck's model doesn't explain gender differences. The explanation does however have face validity; it's an account of dissolution many people can relate to from personal experience or knowledge of others.

Duck doesn't explain why dissatisfaction occurs, as his theory starts where the dissatisfaction has already set in. In this way, it's an incomplete explanation of dissolution. Also Duck's theory is culturally specific and doesn't relate to non-Western collectivist cultures, for example those that favour arranged marriages.

There is also an associated reference to a real-life observation that fits in well here – the use of cosmetics by females to alter appearance for sociobiological ends.

The student also balances their answer with some criticism of the approach that includes pertinent reference to reductionism.

This material on Duck's model of dissolution is similarly impressive. It contains a great deal of embedded IDA material concerning the theory's gender bias. This is achieved through a use of well-focused research material; again, a balanced evaluation is created, this time by reference to the explanation's face validity that clearly explains the point.

The final paragraph makes a good point about the model not accounting for why relationships turn sour and then ends on another pertinent IDA point, this time concerning the model's cultural relevance.

Strong answer: overall comment

Together, the responses to parts (a) and (b) form an excellent, balanced answer, made possible by the cohesive and focused use of material that has been well selected. This would be a clear Grade A.

Question 2

Outline and evaluate research into the influence of culture on romantic relationships.
[**25 marks** (2009 onwards)] [**24 marks** (2012 onwards)]

- The mark breakdown here would be 9 marks (8 marks from 2012) for the outline of research and 16 marks for the evaluation. Therefore, most time and effort, at a ratio of 2 to 1, should be spent compiling the evaluation.
- In exams before 2012, questions in this area wouldn't ask specifically about 'romantic relationships', but would be framed in more general terms, asking about 'the nature of relationships in different cultures'. However, your answer to such a question can focus entirely on romantic relationships and you could bring in any of the material on pp. 40–3.

- The term research doesn't just involve studies, but also covers explanations/theories/models, as they would have been formed from research studies. You could, therefore, address theoretical aspects, such as individualistic versus collectivist cultures, as well as focusing on actual research studies that have investigated the influence of culture on romantic relationships.
- Relevant IDA points could be centred on culturally based issues, such as the dangers of cultural bias when reaching conclusions or using methodologies to research cultural groupings for which they are not appropriate.
- Evaluation based on methodological considerations would be appropriate here too, as the question's main focus is on research.

Average answer

Research into relationships in different cultures cuts across different religions, economic systems and forms of society. Studies show that there are higher divorce rates in Western cultures and this may be because standards of living are comparatively higher and thus Westerners are used to being satisfied. Therefore, getting divorced may be culturally acceptable if it's seen as part of an initiative to gain a better standard of life with a different partner. This suggests Westerners are more selfish and put themselves first. Also, as divorce is more acceptable in Western cultures, when relationships have problems, it's seen as okay to end it rather than try to fix it as in other cultures, where there'd be pressures to keep the relationship going.

In cultures where arranged marriages occur, divorce rates are lower. This may occur because individuals don't have the freedom of choice to end relationships. Religion plays a part here in creating norms where divorce isn't a real option. In cultures with arranged marriages, there are pressures from outside the marriage too, such as from the extended family. Indeed, these types of marriages are seen as marriages between whole families, not just between two individuals; therefore, divorce isn't an individual's choice, as family honour is at stake and pressures are greater to stay together. People in a poor relationship will work at it harder and longer than ☞

This answer does focus on the question, i.e. the influence of culture on romantic relationships, mainly by concentrating on different attitudes towards divorce and analysing why different attitudes may exist. This is an acceptable strategy, but it isn't carried out very effectively, as there is an almost total absence of any identifiable research studies. The term 'research' isn't limited to just studies; it also includes theories and explanations, as they will have emerged from research studies, but even so, the rather general and basic statements contained in this answer means it doesn't gain access to the higher mark bands.

those in a Western equivalent relationship, as they don't want to disappoint or offend other family members. Individual happiness from relationships isn't seen as important as in Western cultures and indeed comes second to the needs and happiness of the overall family.

Non-Western cultures don't tend to be as economically rich as Western ones and therefore individuals can't get divorced as they can't afford to live without each other, especially females who probably don't have access to paid employment. Also, divorced females in these cultures will find it hard to remarry, as they are seen as 'tarnished goods' and not socially acceptable as marriage partners.

It's difficult to compare relationships from different cultures, because there are so many different cultures, and so to divide them up into Western and non-Western or collectivist versus individualistic cultures may be oversimplistic and not give a true picture. Also a lot of the research into this area is carried out using questionnaires, which may be producing idealized answers or socially desirable answers and thus again doesn't give a true picture of what people really feel. What research also tends to do is to produce averages of what people are like or do, but this doesn't reveal the wide-ranging individual differences there are in relationships. Instead, it just produces a stereotype of what a 'typical' relationship is like in a given culture.

One cultural stereotype that can be considered simplistic is the idea that relationships in Western cultures are formed voluntarily because of love, while in non-Western collectivist cultures relationships, they are arranged as economic unions between families. However, research studies have demonstrated in China that a main reason for getting married was because of love and, as China is a non-Western culture, it illustrates the fact that it's extremely difficult to generalize such statements.

What would have made this answer better would have been the use of relevant research, both as descriptive and evaluative material. There is a wealth of such material, including theoretical work by Gupta and Singh, and Moghaddam, as well as specific studies, like that by Vandello and Cohen (2003), who found that women in non-Western cultures have less influence and power in relationships than their Western counterparts and are expected to remain in poor relationships, as not to do so would be dishonourable.

The student does attempt some methodological criticisms, and while they are pertinent, again they could have been much more effective, e.g. by explaining what is meant by 'idealized' and 'socially desirable' answers in this topic area. For instance, people of different cultures may feel a need to provide answers that conform to their cultural norms rather than give true answers.

There is also a lack of specific, embedded IDA material; for instance, they could have commented on the cultural bias of researchers in viewing other cultural practices as being inherently inferior to their own, or on the use of methodologies in cultures they were not designed or standardized for.

Average answer: overall comment

In the light of the comments above (in particular, the occasional drift away from the question, and evaluation that is not always developed or effective), this answer would be worth around a Grade C.

Strong answer

Most research into relationships focuses on Western culture and, as such, is culturally biased. However, some studies have examined differences between cultures. Moghaddam (1993) points out that people of Western cultures are more individualistic, while non-Westerners are more collectivist, and this affects how relationships are formed, perceived and maintained. Relationships in Western cultures also tend to be voluntary. Reasons for this include people's greater social and geographical mobility, and the urban nature of Western society. This creates lots of chances to meet new people, and people therefore have a greater ability to select those they wish to be in relationships with. Non-Western cultures tend to be less urban, with less mobility, and so fewer new people are met. For this reason, it often falls on older family members to arrange marriages for their children.

In Western cultures, individuals base decisions on whether to pursue relationships on their own individual needs, while in collectivist cultures, decisions are based on the needs of whole families. Takano (1999) studied differences between individualist and collectivist cultures, finding how change was perceived to be an important factor. Americans embrace and value change, including change in relationships, especially if it's seen as leading to personal gain. This may explain their relatively high divorce rate. Japanese culture on the other hand tends to favour continuity and stability, including that within relationships and thus have a much lower divorce rate. However, this study only represented two cultures and may not therefore be representative of other individualistic and collectivist cultures.

Ho (1986) argued that Western cultures place more emphasis on love and romance, while other cultures form relationships on the basis of responsibility and family needs, suggesting a different cultural basis to relationships. Moore and Leung (2001) compared native Australians to Chinese immigrants to Australia, finding Australian men had more relationships than Chinese-Australian men and Australian women valued romance more than Australian men, while romance was valued equally between Chinese-Australian men and women. This implies different groups, or sub-cultures, have different views of romance, though the results are only applicable to Australian sub-cultures. ☞

This is a strong opening, focusing immediately on research, as the questions requires, and already notching up IDA marks by bringing in the issue of cultural bias.

The answer has a wide-ranging scope with material being clearly expressed and supported with reasonably detailed psychological content. Most points made strike a good balance in their ratio of descriptive to evaluative material, reflecting the allocation of AO1 and AO2 marks.

This is an impressive coverage of relationships in different cultures. The description is detailed, with impressive explanatory detail and evaluative comments.

Gupta and Singh (1982) found the idea that Western marriages were superior wasn't supported. Indeed, love and liking decreased over time in voluntary marriages, while love and liking grew in those in arranged marriages, which tends to support the idea that parents 'know best' who is compatible for their children, while Westerners can be 'blinded by love' when choosing partners. In comparison, Xiaohe and Whyte (1990) found women who had chosen to be in 'love' marriages in China were happier than those in traditional arranged marriages, though the different results gained here may have been influenced by the rapid and huge social and economic changes occurring in China. There is also some difficulty in comparing satisfaction rates when measurements like divorce rates are used. The USA, with a preponderance of voluntary marriages, has a divorce rate of 55% compared to 1% in India, where there's a lot of arranged marriages. This seems to suggest arranged marriages are superior, but it is less culturally acceptable to get divorced in India, so there will be more pressure from families to keep bad relationships together to avoid bringing shame on the family. In practice, too, it would be difficult for women to survive economically outside of marriage, as job opportunities may not exist for women. This demonstrates that direct comparisons between cultures may be difficult as the methods of assessing relationships are subject to different influences within different cultures, which confuses results and any conclusions drawn.

This student's use of evaluation is well elaborated, adding further evaluative points to improve the quality of the answer. For example, the point made about the difficulty in finding ways of comparing the quality of relationships in different cultures is built up effectively in this way.

This answer is superior to the 'Average answer' by making greater and more effective use of more focused and identifiable research. This ranges from the theoretical work of Moghaddam, through to specific studies such as that of Gupta and Singh, with further research studies used as a form of comparison, e.g. Xiaohe and Whyte's contradictory findings. There is also a greater degree of pertinent IDA commentary; indeed, the answer starts and finishes with such material.

Strong answer: overall comment

This is a very well informed and well-written essay, which would be worth a clear Grade A.

Question 3

Part (a)

Outline the influence of childhood on adult relationships. **[4 marks]**

- In this first part of question 3, only descriptive (AO1) material is required; evaluation would gain no marks and would just waste valuable exam time better spent gaining credit elsewhere.

- This part of the question has quite a specific focus – the influence that childhood has on adult relationships – so you mustn't stray away from this focus, e.g. by including material on peer relations, which wouldn't be relevant here.

Average answer

Childhood is important as it affects the relationships you have in later life as an adult. This has been shown in research. We have lots of relationships in childhood, with the relationships with parents being the most important, though relationships to siblings, peers and significant others are important too.

Ainsworth famously showed that children form different types of relationships in childhood that are dependent on the quality of interactions that they have with primary caregivers. Some psychologists believe that we continue these types of attachments into adulthood, though there is other research that argues that adult relationships can be of a different quality to those we had in childhood. It depends on the circumstances.

This answer is disorganized and unfocused, with the student simply failing to engage properly with the question. The first sentence tells us very little and could almost have been taken from the wording of the question. The comment about research is promising, as what research tells us would have been a valid way of earning credit, but the student doesn't say what research has found in this area. There then follow some unconnected comments about other types of relationships and some material on Ainsworth, possibly remembered from AS developmental psychology. However, the answer does end with some relevant comments about the association between early attachment types and later relationships, and whether there is continuity between them. There is just about enough material to merit 2 marks.

Strong answer

The continuity hypothesis argues that early relationships with primary caregivers provide the foundations on which later adult relationships are based. Young children are perceived as forming an internal working model from their relationship with their primary caregiver. This model gives an individual a view of self, for instance as a likeable person, as well as a view of others, such as whether people are trustworthy or not. Children also develop an attachment style from their early relationships, such as a secure or insecure attachment type, and these are seen as being replicated in later relationships. For instance, a child with a secure attachment style goes on to form warm, loving and secure relationships as an adult.

This is an admirable answer for many reasons. It is of the right length for the mark allocation and incorporates a concise, informative style that allows a lot of relevant information to be conveyed. The answer is also accurate and clearly expressed, with no ambiguities, and the points made are sufficiently developed to merit being awarded the full 4 marks.

Part (b)

Outline sex differences in parental investment. [**5 marks** (2009 onwards)] [**4 marks** (2012 onwards)]

- Here the focus falls on evolutionary theory and specifically on sex differences in parental investment. So, focus on this quite precise requirement so your answer is creditworthy. Prior to 2012, questions will be phrased in more general terms (see Examiners' notes, p. 32).

- As with part (a), only descriptive material is required; evaluation would gain no marks.
- Again, the allocation of marks is relatively low, so you should take care not to write more than what is needed to gain those marks. About 100 to 120 words would be sufficient.

Average answer

Evolutionary theory is an explanation of how behaviour has arisen through the process of natural selection. This is where behaviours that are advantageous help individuals survive into adulthood and thus reproduce and pass their genes for that particular behaviour onto their children. Over generations, this behaviour becomes more widespread throughout the population and can even become a characteristic of a species. So, because males and females have different priorities, gender-based differences in parental behaviour have evolved. Females know they're the mother of their children, whereas males aren't sure they're the father. This means males are more likely to desert to chase after another possible pregnancy and they have more chance to do this when fertilization is internal. It's difficult to test evolutionary theory, though, because, as evolution occurred in the past, it's very retrospective in its explanations and therefore difficult to falsify.

This student has started with a clear description of how evolution occurs and demonstrates a good level of knowledge of this. However, there's no need for this type of introduction to evolutionary theory; the question specifically asks for an outline of sex differences in parental investment. Unfortunately, this type of answer occurs all too often.

The answer only starts earning marks at this point. The material on desertion is especially relevant, with a little elaboration evident about internal fertilization. Unfortunately, the student then wanders away from the requirements of the question by providing an evaluative comment about evolutionary theory. The command word in this question is 'outline', which means to provide a description; anything other than this isn't creditworthy.

Strong answer

An evolutionary explanation of parental investment concerns the difference between sex gametes and parental certainty. Males' investment is smaller than females, as they can produce lots of sperm over a long period of time, incurring few costs in the way of time or energy. However, males can never be sure of paternity, and so their best strategy is to mate with as many females as often as possible. Females, on the other hand are certain of maternity as fertilization is internal. Females also have a much larger investment, as they produce relatively few eggs over a shorter period, and also have the cost of pregnancy and nursing. A female's best strategy, therefore, is to be picky and select the best possible mate for her and her potential offspring.

There are a lot of good aspects to this answer. All the material is relevant and accurate, with a lot of detail being contained within a minimum of words. The candidate introduces the focus of the answer succinctly (i.e. sex gametes and parental certainty) and then goes on to elaborate this, first in terms of males and then in terms of females. So, the answer fits the top band of marks, even though there is some scope for further elaboration of points. For example, it's not really explained what females selecting the 'best possible mate' means; the student could have gone on here to talk about selection in terms of males' ability to provide resources. Marks aren't taken away for omissions, but including this would have made the answer even more impressive.

Part (c)

Evaluate research studies concerning the influence of culture on romantic relationships. **[16 marks]**

- The final part of question 3 requires evaluative material only, so you should resist the urge to describe research studies first before evaluating them, as the description would earn no marks.
- The question refers specifically to *research studies*, so your focus should be on those, and not on a wider scope of theories/explanations/models.
- In exams before 2012, questions in this area wouldn't ask specifically about 'romantic relationships', but would be framed in more general terms, asking about 'the nature of relationships in different cultures'. However, your answer to such a question can focus entirely on romantic relationships and you could bring in any of the material on pp. 40–3.

- Appropriate evaluation could take the form of what research studies inform us about the influence of culture on romantic relationships. This is best achieved by placing an evaluative statement at the beginning and end of a point, a tactic known as 'topping and tailing'. For example: '*Research suggests arranged marriages can have a high content of love to them.* Gupta and Singh (1982) found loving and liking for partners grew over a 10-year period for those in arranged marriages. As they also found loving and liking declined in a similar period for those in voluntary marriages, *this implies that arranged marriages are more satisfying long-term.*'
- IDA points could pertinently centre on the risk of cultural bias and the inappropriate use of methodologies designed upon and for specific cultures.

Average answer

In Western cultures, people are generally free to choose one another, while in non-Western cultures, it's more normal to have marriages arranged by your family. Arranged marriages tend to be of a more permanent nature and can be considered more of a union between families than between partners. This can cause tensions in multicultural societies, like Britain, where tensions and conflicts occur, because young people value individual choice more, with older generations favouring traditional arranged marriages.

Divorce rates differ between cultures too, with Western cultures having higher rates. However, this might not reflect less satisfaction with relationships, but just that it's easier to get divorced in Western cultures. McKenry and Price (1995) found that in cultures where females have become more independent, divorce rates have risen; this suggests that the lower divorce rates often seen in non-individualistic cultures are not a reflection of happy marriages, but of male dominance. Umadevi *et al.* (1992) examined Indian female student preferences for love marriages and arranged marriages. Arranged marriages were perceived positively, as long as the two intended partners consented. However, love marriages were preferred too, so long as parents approved, illustrating the importance of whole family opinions in Indian society. ☛

It's a good idea to practise these 'evaluation only' types of question as a regular part of your learning, as you won't have come across them during your AS year. The question is focused on research studies and, specifically, on *evaluation* of them. However, this answer only occasionally achieves this. This first paragraph, although accurate, has nothing to do with research studies and, as such, gains no credit.

This paragraph starts with another non-creditworthy point about divorce levels, but the answer becomes creditworthy when discussing the validity of divorce level findings.

Three studies about divorce rates and free-choice versus arranged marriages are then made, which all contain some non-creditworthy descriptive material, but a good level of creditworthy content too where the studies are evaluated in terms of what they suggest.

Zaidi and Shuraydi (2002) performed a study where they interviewed Muslim women who originated from Pakistan, but were raised in Canada, about how they felt about arranged marriages. Most preferred love marriages of their choice, but their elders, especially their fathers, were very opposed, showing the potential for conflicts within cultural groups that form minorities within more dominant cultures.

It might be considered unethical to question people about the quality of their relationships, as this could cause distress, especially in relationships where there were tensions. Such research could also be considered socially sensitive when questioning women's attitudes to relationships in male-dominated cultures. If males of a culture didn't like the answers women were giving, it could lead to tensions and retributions.

The answer ends with a fairly well-constructed ethical point concerning the possible pitfalls of questioning people about their attitudes to their own relationships; in terms of this question, this is perfectly acceptable.

Average answer: overall comment

The student has not really made their evaluation work effectively, which has limited the AO2 marks and made this answer worth around a Grade C only. A better approach would have been to create a commentary on the degree of research support for these claims. Evaluation of methodological points concerning research in this area would also have been advisable.

Strong answer

Research studies conducted into relationships tend to be centred on Western cultures and may not be applicable to other cultures. For instance, Lee's theory of relationship dissolution was based on a survey of 112 break-ups of non-marital, romantic relationships. However, such relationships would rarely be found in non-Western cultures, and indeed the only non-marital relationships occurring would be pre-marital ones that were strictly supervised by chaperones.

Another problem with research into relationships in different cultures is that of an imposed etic, where Western research methodologies are used to assess relationships in other countries when they may not be suited for that use.

Argyle et al. (1986) found that different rules of relationships operated in different cultures. However, a problem with studies such as this is that the list of rules is drawn up by Western psychologists and so reflects things that are considered important in those cultures. As a result, rules that are specific to a culture (e.g. Japan) may not be included.

Practical applications based on psychological research can have positive implications for society, but only if based on appropriate methodology – otherwise, psychological applications can have a negative impact on people.

The dominant research method in this area is that of questionnaires and there is a risk therefore of socially desirable answers being given, where people answer in terms of what their culture would expect them to say. Indeed, it is hard to imagine people giving opinions that go against their cultural values. The other side of this is researcher bias, where investigators interpret data from such studies in terms of their own biased cultural expectations and norms. Also, most cultural groups are transitory and even accurate research studies may, therefore, quickly go out of date. This is especially so in multicultural societies, where the constant mix of peoples and their cultural values can create great changes very rapidly in the nature of relationships.

Cultural similarities in romantic relationships suggest an adaptive significance for romantic love. Pinker (2008) claims that romantic love evolved to promote health benefits in long-term partnerships and to promote reproductive opportunities. Jankowiak and Fischer ☞

Many candidates would focus on the formation of romantic relationships to answer this question, but the question is wider than that; the *breakdown* of relationships is equally relevant and so the material covered in this answer is absolutely appropriate. The student begins by pointing out that much research in this area is Western based and may, therefore, not be applicable to other cultures, giving a relevant, well-explained example as elaboration.

The theme is then developed into a discussion about an imposed etic, which is an admirable use of a psychological concept and its terminology.

The answer continues with a specific discussion of methodological points, done in a way that is very pertinent to the question. Many candidates make methodological points that are too general to gain credit.

(1992) provided support for this claim of love being universal with their finding that romantic love existed in 90% of nearly 200 cultures studied.

This final paragraph offers an evolutionary perspective from which to interpret that there are cultural *similarities* in the experience of romantic love. This adds to the IDA content for this question. The inclusion of the Jankowiak and Fischer evidence adds evidence to Pinker's assertion, so offers important elaboration for the point.

Strong answer: overall comment

An excellent answer, with a good deal of scope, centred on problems associated with conducting cross-cultural research into relationships. The length of this answer is about the maximum that most students could produce in the time available. The IDA content of this answer is well embedded into the cultural nature of the topic material, e.g. the discussion about the danger of an imposed etic and cultural bias, as well as the final paragraph offering an evolutionary perspective on cultural similarities in romantic love. All in all, as the content is accurate, clearly expressed and concise, with well-informed description and effective evaluation, this is a clear Grade A standard essay.

Example Paper 2

Question 1

Part (a)

Outline the influence of childhood on adult relationships. **[5 marks** (2009 onwards)**] [4 marks** (2012 onwards)**]**

- Part (a) of this question has a narrow focus – the influence of childhood on adult relationships – although material on adolescence would also be creditworthy.
- The question also specifically asks for an outline, so only descriptive material should be offered, and not evaluative or analytical material, which wouldn't earn any marks.

- As only 5 marks are on offer (4 marks from 2012), you should limit the answer to about 100 to 120 words – or about five minutes of writing time. There is no point writing more than that – however good the material – as it will not earn extra credit.

Average answer

Children have a number of relationships – with parents, siblings, peers and significant others. Each of these affects our later adult relationships in different ways, but peers become more important, because as we get older, we spend more time with them and are more influenced by them than by parents, who had a larger previous influence.

Peer relationships in adolescence become a kind of training ground for adult relationships, especially romantic ones. Adolescents who are rejected by their peers go on to have the highest levels of unsuccessful adult relationships. However, this is only correlational evidence and doesn't show causality – for instance, the quality of earlier attachments with parents may be playing a more dominant role.

There are two negative criticisms of this answer:
- Quite a lot of the material isn't focused on the question, and only those parts of answers that directly answer questions will gain credit. For example, detailing the different types of relations individuals have doesn't earn any marks.
- The second half of the answer is better focused, especially the comments relating to peer relationships as a training ground and those about individuals rejected by their peers. Unfortunately, however, the answer strays into evaluation with the (albeit accurate) comment about correlational evidence, whereas the question only asks for descriptive material.

Strong answer

The most important childhood influence on adult relationships is relationships with peers, as peers play a critical role in individuals becoming independent adults, helping them to develop the social skills required for adult relationships. Research has found that peers influence adult relationships, because both the type and quality of adolescent relationships relate to the type and quality of adult relationships. Kirchler *et al.* found that adolescents who don't develop peer relationships may have difficulties engaging in adult relationships later.

Connelly and Goldberg (1999) found that the level of intimacy in peer relationships laid the foundations for the degree of intimacy in young adult relationships. Simpson *et al.* (2007) found that adolescents who were closer to their friends at 16 were more emotionally attached to their partners in adulthood.

This is an accurate answer, with the student making an initial statement that relationships with peers are the most important influence on adult relationships. This is a perfectly acceptable way of interpreting the question. The answer goes on to outline how peers influence the development of social skills needed for adult relationships, detailing research findings about specific influences, such as about the type and quality of adolescent/adult relationships and the level of intimacy. With such good use of research evidence to substantiate the points made, this answer would be worth full marks.

Part (b)

*Outline and evaluate **one** theory of relationship maintenance.* **[20 marks]**

- This part of the question calls for both descriptive (AO1) and evaluative (AO2) content, but is heavily weighted in favour of evaluation, with only 4 marks available for the outline, compared to 16 for the evaluation. (How do we know it is 4 marks of AO1? Because there are always 16 marks of AO2 available per complete question, and as part (a) was all AO1, then all the AO2 marks must be loaded into part (b), i.e. 16 marks of AO2 and just 4 marks of AO1.) Possibly the best approach would be to describe one theory briefly and then move quickly on to the more important evaluative material.
- Remember to write about one theory only. If more than one theory were offered, all would be marked, but only the best one credited.

- Evaluation could be achieved by considering the degree of research support the explanation has and/or by making comparisons with other theories in order to draw out strengths and weaknesses.
- Pertinent IDA points could be built around the gender bias of some theories/research, plus the opportunities for practical applications in relationship guidance.
- If offering evaluation based on methodology, take care not to orientate the answer towards evaluating studies, rather than theory, which is the question's main focus.

Average answer

One theory of relationship maintenance is that of social exchange theory (SET), which sees people as fundamentally selfish. People are seen as perceiving their feelings for others in terms of profits, that is the rewards gained from relationships minus the costs. The greater the rewards and lower the costs, then the greater the profit, and, therefore, the greater the desire to maintain the relationship. Because the commitments to relationships and the interactions necessary to conduct them are time and energy consuming, the theory believes that, for a relationship to be maintained, it must exceed the costs. This is therefore an economic theory, which purely explains relationship maintenance in terms of maximizing profits and minimizing costs, with the social exchange component being the mutual exchange of rewards and costs between partners, such as sex and freedoms given up. Rewards are seen as calculated by making two assessments: (1) the comparison level, where rewards are compared to costs to assess profits, and (2) the comparison level for alternative relationships, where rewards and costs are compared against perceived rewards and costs for possible alternative relationships.

Murstein found the theory mainly applies to people who 'keep score', with such scorekeepers being suspicious and insecure individuals, which suggests the theory only suits those relationships that are lacking confidence ☞

Here we have an unbalanced answer in terms of the requirements of the question. Only 4 marks are on offer for an outline of a theory of relationship maintenance, but the student gives an outline that is far too long. The material offered is all relevant, detailed and accurate, but valuable time has been spent compiling too much material that just wasn't necessary.

and mutual trust. Sedikides (2005) also criticizes the theory by suggesting people are capable of being unselfish and doing things for others without expecting anything in return. Sedikides believes individuals encourage and support their partners when they're faced with failure and other stressful life events. This means that the view of humans as just out for what they can get is far too simplistic and inaccurate to be true. The theory can also be accused of being gender biased, as it's more likely to be men who are out for a profit.

In this second, evaluative part of the answer, the material is relevant, reasonably detailed and accurate. It's also well expressed in an informative, concise manner. However, there just isn't enough of it to merit the 16 AO2 marks on offer. The quality of the answer is also brought down by the lack of pertinent IDA material; there is one rudimentary comment about the theory's gender bias, but without any real explanation or evidence as to why this might be so. The answer would have benefited from more evaluation in terms of the degree of research support and other analytical material, such as the fact that research has tended to concentrate on short-term consequences of relationships, rather than more important long-term maintenance.

Average answer: overall comment

It may be a result of bad planning rather than lack of knowledge, but the inappropriate detail and lack of balance has resulted in this being at a Grade C standard, rather than a higher grade, which the student might have hoped for.

Strong answer

Equity theory sees individuals as motivated to achieve fairness in relationships and to feel dissatisfied with unfairness. Maintenance of relationships is therefore achieved through balance and stability, by individuals putting into relationships as much as they receive back from them. When inequity is perceived within a relationship, it offers up an opportunity for adjustments to be made so that a return to equity can be achieved. Thus equity theory sees relationships being maintained by a repeating cycle of balance and imbalance.

Canary and Stafford (1992) provided research support for equity theory with their Relationship Maintenance Strategies Measure, which they used to assess the degree of equity in romantic relationships. A link was found between degree of perceived equity and the prevalence of maintenance strategies, which implies equitable relationships are maintained. Dainton (2003) provided further research support by finding that those in relationships of perceived inequity had low relationship satisfaction, but were motivated to return to an equitable state to maintain their relationships. This suggests that equity is a main factor in relationship satisfaction and maintenance.

Equity theory however, isn't a valid explanation of relationship maintenance, at least not in a conscious fashion, as Argyle (1977) found people in close relationships don't think in terms of rewards and costs, unless they feel dissatisfied. Another criticism is that equity is more important to females. Hoschchild and Machung (1989) found that women do most work in making relationships equitable, suggesting the theory isn't applicable to both genders. Moghaddam (1993) also suggested equity theory doesn't apply to all cultures, as he found American students prefer equity, but European students prefer equality, implying the theory reflects the values of US society.

An excellent answer. Only 4 marks are available for the outline of a theory of relationship maintenance, and this student writes just the right amount of relevant, accurate material to secure these marks without wasting valuable exam time by overproducing material.

The evaluation is then achieved in high-level fashion in two distinct ways:
- by the use of research which both supports the theory, as in the case of Canary and Stafford (1992) and Dainton (2003), as well as that opposing it, as by Argyle (1977)
- by embedded use of IDA material concerning the theory's application across genders and cultures – IDA material like this, which truly engages with the topic at hand, scores at the highest level.

Strong answer: overall comment

This answer is concise yet very effective and is clearly worth a clear Grade A.

Question 2

Discuss the relationship between sexual selection and human reproductive behaviour.
[25 marks (2009 onwards)**] [24 marks** (2012 onwards)**]**

- 'Discuss', in this context, means to outline and describe the relationship between sexual selection and human reproductive behaviour, with 9 marks (8 marks from 2012) available for the descriptive content and 16 for the evaluative content.
- There is a wealth of relevant material that could be used to answer this question, so you would need to make a decision as to what to include. Two basic strategies suggest themselves: first, an answer of depth, where a narrow focus is created, but with a lot of detail (e.g. concentrating an answer on sexual dimorphism, the difference in male and female characteristics), or alternatively, a wider-ranging answer with less detail (e.g. focusing on various elements of male and female attractiveness, such as resource richness and physical attractiveness).

- As the evaluation scores more marks, more time and effort should be directed towards that, e.g. by considering the degree of research support, as well as embedding IDA material into relevant aspects of evolutionary theory, such as its reductionist nature.
- Finally, the question requires you to focus on human reproductive behaviour and not on that of non-humans. A little such research could possibly be used, if only to draw out pertinent comments about the problems of generalizing findings to humans.

Average answer

There are two basic types of sexual selection. Firstly, intra-sexual selection, which refers to competition between members of the same sex for access to members of the opposite sex, such as males fighting over a woman. The idea is the winner will prove himself the most dominant one and will get access to an opportunity for sexual reproduction, whereas the losers won't have as many, if any, chances for similar opportunities.

The second type of sexual selection is known as inter-sexual selection and differs from intra-sexual selection as this time it refers to females selecting from the available pool of males who they would like to mix their genes with in reproduction. The females want to pick the best male that they can, because then their children will have his strong genes and this will increase their chances of surviving until adulthood and then reproducing themselves so the genes get passed on again.

With intra-sexual selection, males will especially compete for females who they see as being young and pretty, because these qualities are seen as advertising the female's fertility. Therefore, she will be worth pursuing, as it's more likely she'll get pregnant and reproduce his genes for him. While males are competing against each other for access to females, they're also ☞

The material that this student presents is relevant and is generally accurate throughout, so this is by no means a bad answer, but there is room for lots of improvement. First, the student has a very long-winded writing style, using a lot of words, and valuable exam time, to say relatively little. They should try and develop a more concise, informative style that allows them to express their points more clearly and with more detail. At times, the answer also reads like a series of unconnected points and so lacks an elaborated narrative that often characterizes a good essay.

The result is that the answer is unbalanced; only one-third of the marks are for the outline, as compared to two-thirds for the evaluation, but the majority of this answer is descriptive. It should be the other way round. This is a common mistake in exam answers – it probably happens as students tend to write their descriptions first and spend too long doing it. The solution is to write essay-style answers as a regular feature of your learning, making a plan of points to include before writing the essay.

demonstrating to females their reproductive ability through strength. Not only would this get passed on to her children, he could also use his strength to protect her and her children from harm. But females are also looking for males to demonstrate their ability to provide resources, with which he could support her and her children. Research has shown that females like resources in men and for them to be ambitious in trying to get resources. Research has shown that men like youth and prettiness too, backing up the idea that males and females are looking for different things. Men also like a certain waist-to-hip ratio, as this is another indicator of fertility in women. Penton-Voak did some research that showed females like facial symmetry in males, this is because it indicates developmental stability. Some individuals are not as able to compete as others and will have to lower their demands to get access to mating opportunities, such as women who are older. Research has shown that women are less picky in their mate selections when they get older.

Males are about 15% bigger than females; this is called sexual dimorphism and is a secondary sexual characteristic, which is an honest indicator of a male's reproductive fitness. This is because a fit male can show the physical prowess that his bigger levels of testosterone allow. Research has shown this to be related to immune system functioning, with fit males having good immune system functioning, and so if a female picks such a fit male, her children will get that quality too and that will help them to survive into adulthood and reproduce.

Research into sexual selection often involves animals, like peacocks, and the results might not be true of humans. Evolutionary theory is also reductionist, because it doesn't consider non-biological influences. Evolutionary theory can also be considered determinist, as it sees all of our behaviour as being determined by evolution.

As it is, our student focuses on intra- and intersexual selection, which is fine as a strategy, and they certainly show that they have a thorough grasp of the material. Although the material could be better expressed, there is enough of it, with sufficient breadth, to merit getting all the AO1 marks available. However, this has been achieved by limiting the amount of time left to write the evaluation with its 16 marks available.

Sadly, the evaluation presented here is not of a high standard. There isn't enough of it and, especially compared to the 'Strong answer' on pp. 70–1, it is less incisive and effective. When evidence is used, it is generally not used successfully. For instance, the comment about females liking facial symmetry in males because it indicates developmental stability could have been improved by then saying that this quality would be passed on to sons, thus increasing their reproductive potential.

Finally, the use of IDA points reads like something tagged on at the end, without it really engaging with the material in a meaningful way. Compare this student's superficial comments about reductionism to the far superior way the 'Strong answer' uses the concept to complement the point being made. Again, this skill needs to be learned and honed by regular practice as part of a systematic revision process.

Average answer: overall comment

This answer has been let down by ineffective evaluation and a general lack of IDA development; as such, it would be worth around a Grade C.

Strong answer

There is a difference between male and female human reproductive behaviours, and this occurs because of males and females being prone to different selective pressures. With sexual selection, characteristics are sought in the opposite gender that are indicative of reproductive success, and different characteristics are sought because of anisogamy, where there are differences in the sex gametes of males and females and the degree of certainty of parenthood that both genders have.

Males produce lots of small, highly mobile sperm and can do this fairly regularly over a long period of time and thus hypothetically have many opportunities for reproduction. Females, on the over hand, produce relatively small numbers of larger eggs over a shorter period of time. Females will only have approximately 300 opportunities to reproduce and have the additional costs of bearing and nurturing children. Therefore, each potential reproduction is more valuable to females than it is to males. The other important factor is that females are always certain of the maternity of her children, that she is raising her own genes. Males can never be certain of this – there's always a possibility they're raising another male's genes. Therefore, a male's best strategy is to have as much sex with as many fertile females as possible and only to become bonded to a single or a few females, if by doing so it decreases the chances of cuckoldry. This creates intrasexual competition between males and polygamy, a system where a male mates with several females, preferably who exhibit signs of fertility. A female's best strategy is to be choosy by indulging in intersexual competition and selecting males who display genetic fitness and to be reluctant, encouraging males to participate in lengthy courtship rituals, which compels them to invest time and effort in securing a reproductive opportunity and also gets them to display their ability to provide resources.

Dunbar and Waynforth (1995) found that males valued physical attractiveness and youth in females, supporting the idea that males seek fertility in females. The same study found females value financial capacity in males and ambition and industriousness, supporting the idea that females seek males who are research rich and able to provide for them and their children. The study found these tendencies were cross-cultural, data ☞

This student provides a thoroughly clear and accurate account of the differences between males and females in terms of sexual selection and how it affects their reproductive capability. The difference between sex cells is detailed and leads into a description of differences in reproductive strategies, as predicted by evolutionary theory.

This part of the answer clearly earns the 9 AO1 marks on offer (8 marks from 2012) for descriptive material. If anything, there is slightly too much material, the student could have offered a little less and still have got all the marks without eating into the time left to spend on the evaluation, where 16 marks are available.

being collected from 33 countries, suggesting the traits are genetically determined with an evolutionary value. Although evolutionary theory is retrospective, telling us how things may have come about, studies like this provide a useful methodology to test the theory, by making predictions based on evolutionary principles and then seeing if they exist in actuality. This addresses the criticism made by some that evolutionary theory isn't scientific due to it being unfalsifiable. Dunbar and Waynforth's findings were backed up by Davis (1990), who found from personal advertisements that males seek health and attractiveness, symbols of fertility, while offering wealth and resources, qualities indicating genetic fitness that females seek. Conversely, females sought resources and status, while offering beauty and youth, again all in line with evolutionary theory. This, in turn, received further support from Dunbar and Waynforth (1995), also from personal advertisements, who found 42% of males compared to 25% of females sought youthful partners, while 44% of males compared to 22% of females sought physical attractiveness.

Partridge (1980) gave some female fruit flies free mate choice, while others had forced matings with randomly chosen males. Offspring of all matings were assessed for competitive ability by being reared with a fixed number of standard competitors. Offspring of free choice females did best, illustrating how females improve the reproductive success of children by selecting good genes in their partners. How far this is generalizable to humans is debatable, and generalizing animal findings onto humans is reductionist, as removing human relationships from historical and cultural contexts portrays them as no different from non-human relationships. For example, women may obtain resources through men due to being denied direct access to political and economic power.

Fortunately, the student fills their evaluation with a wealth of relevant, detailed material orientated at the points made in the outline. With so much wide-ranging material to draw on in this topic area, they make the sensible decision to concentrate on providing an elaborated evaluation of the idea that males and females seek different things in reproductive partners. This is done by the use of pertinent, accurate material presented with a high degree of clarity, using research evidence in a highly effective manner.

The student also cleverly weaves relevant IDA material into the answer in a seamless manner. The criticism of evolutionary theory being non-scientific due to its unfalsifiable nature is addressed through the idea of testing out evolutionary predictions in the real world.

Then, rather than just making a basic point about animals studies not being generalizable to humans, as many students would, the student expands on this to turn it into a salient point about reductionism with the use of an incisive example about how women obtain resources. The evaluation therefore makes the top band and suffers only very slightly from the student being slightly rushed after overproducing descriptive material in the first part of the answer.

Strong answer: overall comment

Some very effective and elaborated evaluative material pushes this answer to a clear Grade A.

Question 3

Outline and evaluate evolutionary explanations for sex differences in parental investment.
[25 marks (2009 onwards)] **[24 marks** (2012 onwards)]

- For this question, 9 marks are on offer for the outline (8 marks after 2012) and 16 for the evaluation, so most time and effort should be directed at compiling the evaluation.
- In exams prior to 2012, questions about evolutionary explanations of parental investment may not mention 'sex differences' specifically or may include the term as an example only. Either way, you can confidently base your whole essay on sex differences in parental investment.
- With the outline, take care not to be too general and merely describe evolutionary theory; to gain higher marks, you need to focus specifically on how evolutionary theory explains parental investment.

- For the evaluation, an appropriate strategy would be to assess the degree of research support there is for the explanation. This task is made a little easier with this question, as the focus isn't just on humans, so non-human animal studies are equally applicable.
- IDA points could refer to the limitations of the explanation in not considering non-biological influences; this would also give you the opportunity to use alternative theoretical aspects as a means of comparison.

Average answer

Evolutionary theory can be applied to parental behaviour, which is quite closely linked to sexual selection. To start off with, a male isn't certain of being a child's father and research suggests that this uncertainty is true some of the time. If a man thinks a baby looks like him, he'll be more likely to think it is his and contribute more parental resources. He will also be more likely to stick around for the child's upbringing, which he'll be more likely to contribute to as well. He's also more likely to stay in a relationship with the child's mother if he thinks she is faithful to him. There are various ways a male can enhance the chances of a female's fidelity, such as sticking close to her so that other males don't get mating opportunities and being a good, constant source of resources for her and her children, so that she doesn't feel the need to look for an alternative mate. If a male is reasonably certain that his female partner is faithful, this makes him feel he is the father and again is likely to contribute more parental resources. Some research found that if a man wasn't confident he was the father of a child then he would spend less time interacting with the child and less time involved in its education.

For a male, sperm is cheap to supply – that's not so for female eggs – so it suits a male to be more promiscuous and mate freely with as many females as he can. Females are going to be a lot choosier when it comes around ☞

This answer is focused on the question and it is clear the student has knowledge of the topic area. However, the material isn't used very effectively, often being presented in a superficial manner, without much insight into the points being made. The material quoted, although relevant and generally accurate, lacks any real psychological depth, and doesn't convey a sense of detailed knowledge and understanding of the area.

to selecting a partner and there is always the danger that a male will desert her and any children if he has the opportunity, so he can mate elsewhere. This would mean her parental investment would be very large, while his would be minimal. This isn't always the case, though, as in some species females desert first, leaving the male to do all the parental investment – sea horses do this, for example. Generally, though, especially with humans, females invest more, as they are tied to the children through pregnancy and feeding. Each child is a big part of her sexual investment, so it makes sense for her to invest more as a parent into her children – plus she knows they are hers, whereas the male never does. Females will become infertile long before males do, and their mating opportunities are limited also by pregnancies, so again it makes sense for her to invest more as a parent. This isn't always so, though, as research shows males are sometimes the choosier ones. There are fish where the males choose larger females, as they contain more eggs. Perhaps they do this because there isn't that many chances for them to reproduce so it's more important to get it right and invest more as a parent.

If evolutionary theory is correct about parental investment, then male stepfathers – and female stepmothers for that matter – should invest less in their stepchildren as they are certain that they have no genetic relationship to these individuals, and so it wouldn't make evolutionary sense to invest in them. This also means that other relatives, such as grandparents, should invest more if they are certain they are related to children. This therefore means that maternal relatives would invest more than paternal relatives.

Although evolutionary theory provides an explanation of differences in parental investment, it can be considered a deterministic as well as a reductionist explanation. Another criticism of evolutionary explanations is that they aren't falsifiable and therefore cannot be considered scientific.

Material needs to be explained more specifically in terms of the question being answered. For example, evolutionary theory does predict that males will be more promiscuous, but the answer doesn't explain why evolutionary theory predicts this, apart from saying that sperm is cheap to supply. An explanation is needed if the student wants to show their level of understanding more and gain more marks. There is also a need to say how points like this tie in with parental investment, i.e. make the material fit the question, as otherwise the answer reads more like one about sexual selection.

Research quoted tends to be general and difficult to identify specifically; it is also mainly of a descriptive nature. When evaluative points are made, they are not well focused. For instance, the student describes some general research findings about paternal uncertainty and fathers not interacting with children or investing in their education; however, this could have been used much more effectively as evaluation by the simple device of saying 'this suggests that…' or 'this implies that male parental investment is related to the degree of perceived certainty of paternity to a child'.

The student is correct to talk about maternal relatives investing more in children and for the reasons stated; it's a pity, though, that they don't go the logical step further and provide relevant research details. For instance, in the 'Strong answer' on pp. 74–5, research by Nettles (2007) is used very effectively in relation to just this point.

The student finishes their answer by providing a 'shopping list' of IDA points. These could have been developed into much more effective points, but there is no explanation of any of them that conveys a deeper understanding – for instance, the evolutionary explanation of human reproductive behaviour can be seen as reducing complex behaviours like parental investment down to the level of genes, without any reference to learning experiences or cultural influences.

Average answer: overall comment

There is the blueprint for a decent answer here, but to gain higher marks, it would need to convey a deeper level of understanding and use research and IDA points much more effectively. This is worth a Grade C.

Strong answer

Parental investment is investment that increases a child's chances of survival, at the expense of parents' ability to invest in other children, either ones living or yet to be born. Males are never sure of paternity and so their best strategy is to impregnate as many females and therefore spread their parental investment around. Clark and Hatfield (1989) found males are more promiscuous, supporting this notion.

A female's parental investment in each potential reproduction is much larger. She produces relatively few eggs, is fertile for a far shorter period and bears the costs of pregnancy and childrearing. Her best strategy is to indulge in behaviours increasing the survival chances of her children. This is best achieved by selecting genetically fit males as mates. Buss (1989) found females select resource rich, ambitious men, supporting this idea and demonstrating how mate selection by females can enhance their parental investment by increasing the survival chances of their offspring.

Evolutionary theory allows a number of predictions to be made concerning how males and females will act according to their differential parental investments. These then allow the theory to be tested out by examining real-life behaviour. In this way, the theory becomes falsifiable, thus meeting its requirements for a scientifically acceptable theory. For instance, the concept of parental certainty means that with internal fertilization males should be more likely to desert than with external fertilization, as they're less certain of the offspring's paternity with internal fertilization. Gross and Shine (1981) found with internal fertilization that parental care is carried out by females in 86% of species, while with external fertilization parental care is carried out by males in 70% of species, supporting these predictions based on paternal certainty. However, Krebs and Davies (1981) report that it isn't always true that external fertilization leads to increased paternal certainty. In sunfishes, cuckoldry occurs during the female's egg positioning.

The concept of parental certainty is also supported by Nettle (2007), who found that maternal grandparents had more contact with grandchildren than paternal grandparents did and gave a wider range of financial benefits and essential items to newborn grandchildren. This is in line with evolutionary theory, as maternal grandparents are sure of the genetic link to their ☞

The student uses the commendable tactic of outlining a point in a concise, detailed manner, and then providing pertinent research evidence to complement the point and draw out further understanding of the area being discussed. This is achieved in a balanced manner, with evidence for and against being presented. The material used is highly accurate throughout, again elevating the essay to the higher mark bands. The student also cleverly 'signposts' their evaluative conclusions by using phrases such as '*supporting the predictions…*' or '*going against this notion…*'.

grandchildren due to maternal certainty through the mother. The methodology allowed quantitative measures to be taken, which permitted an objective assessment of evolutionary theory predictions, lending the theory scientific validity. However, the study doesn't consider the role of socialization, i.e. that it's a cultural expectation that maternal grandparents will contribute more and have a closer relationship. A possible confounding variable here comes from evolutionary theory, in that males tend to disperse more widely from their parental home, to seek resources and mates, therefore making visits and bonding more difficult for paternal grandparents.

The order of gamete release between genders means that internal fertilization gives males the first chance to desert and leave childrearing to females, while with external fertilization females have first opportunity to desert. In humans, it is true that about 90% of single parent families are female led, supporting this prediction. However, Krebs and Davies (1981) found that males of some fish species release sperm first in a nest and then the female lays her eggs, giving the male the first chance to desert, but actually the males carry out all the childcare while the female deserts, going against this notion.

In species, including humans, where the young are born at an early stage of development or where childcare is intensive, male and female parental pair-bonds should tend to be monogamous and long lasting, to increase the chances of the young's survival. Daly (1979) reports that, in many bird species and some mammals, exclusive, monogamous relationships and biparental care are most apparent, because the males need to contribute to the nurturing of the young to ensure their survival, thus protecting his parental investment and supporting the predictions for monogamy.

There are two good examples of IDA points in this answer:
- commentary on the ability of evolutionary theory to be falsifiable by making predictions that can be tested out (third paragraph on p. 74)
- a more elaborated point about the scientific validity of evolutionary theory that takes in cultural expectations and the idea of a confounding variable based on the approach itself (fourth paragraph).

This is an excellent answer in many respects. There is an appropriate balance of descriptive and evaluative material, accurately reflecting the number of marks available for each: 9 marks for AO1 (8 marks from 2012) compared to 16 for AO2. The answer is well constructed and expressed in a clear, informative and highly focused manner.

Average answer: overall comment

This answer is highly indicative of a candidate who not only knows and understands the topic and communicates it well, but has also practised their essay-writing skills on a regular basis to reach this high level of competence. This is a clear Grade A.

Glossary

Adaptive   Term used to describe an evolved behaviour (or trait) that increases the likelihood of the individual's survival and successful reproduction

Attachment style   The way an individual relates to others in the context of intimate relationships

Autonomic nervous system   That part of the nervous system that maintains the normal functioning of the body's inner environment

Classical conditioning   A form of learning where a neutral stimulus is paired with a stimulus that already produces a response, such that, over time, the neutral stimulus also produces that response

Cognitive dissonance   People experience cognitive dissonance when two (or more) cognitions are inconsistent with each other (i.e. they are dissonant). Because dissonance is an unpleasant experience, the individual is motivated to reduce it

Collectivist cultures   Cultures that value group loyalty, preferring collective to individual decisions; cultures where the needs of the group outweigh the needs of the individual

Comparison level   The comparison between the rewards and costs of a reference (i.e. current) relationship and what we have been used to in the past or believe is appropriate given the nature of the relationship

Comparison level for alternatives   The comparison of the rewards and costs associated with a current relationship and the rewards and costs of possible alternative relationships

Cuckoldry   When a woman deceives her partner into investing in (e.g. providing for, protecting) offspring conceived with another man

Cultural discourse   Patterns of thinking and communication common within a particular culture

Cyber relationships   Relationships formed and conducted over the Internet

Determinism   The philosophical doctrine that an individual's behaviour is shaped or controlled by internal or external forces rather than an individual's will to do something

Deviant behaviour   Actions that violate accepted behaviour within a culture; includes both breaking formal rules or laws (i.e. crime) and informal violations of social norms (e.g. antisocial behaviour)

Environment of evolutionary adaptiveness (EEA)   The environment to which a species is adapted and the set of selection pressures that operated at that time. The EEA is generally regarded to be the African Savannah, sometime between 10 000 and five million years ago

Equity theory   A theory of relationships which stresses that people strive to achieve fairness in their relationships and feel distressed if they perceive unfairness

Ethnocentric   The term used to describe the belief in the pre-eminence of one's own ethnic and cultural group; research may be ethnocentric if it fails to take account of cultural differences

Fitness   A central idea in evolutionary theory, referring to the ability of an organism both to survive and to reproduce

Gametes   Reproductive cells that unite during sexual reproduction to form a new cell called a zygote; in humans, male gametes are sperm and female gametes are ova (eggs)

Halo effect   The idea that if someone has positive attributes such as physical attraction, they are thought to have other positive attributes as well. For example, attractiveness appears to be a particularly important feature that people use when judging the 'quality' of a potential partner

Individualist cultures (individualism)   Cultures where self-interest and individual rights are promoted, rather than the needs and interests of others

Internal working models   An inner representation of the parent–child bond that subsequently becomes an important part of an individual's personality. It serves as a set of expectations about the availability of attachment figures and the likelihood of receiving support from them. This model becomes the basis for all future close relationships during childhood, adolescence and adult life

Intersexual selection   The process whereby a trait gains an advantage because it is attractive to the opposite sex ('inter' = across)

Intrasexual selection   The process whereby a trait gains an advantage because it helps an individual compete with same-sex rivals ('intra' = within)

Investment theory   The theory of relationship maintenance that focuses on the extent to which commitment is determined by investment in the relationship (rather than concentrating solely on satisfaction in relationships)

Longitudinal study   An investigation in which an individual or group of individuals is studied at regular intervals over a relatively long period of time

Matching hypothesis   The view that couples seek to form relationships with the best possible partner they think they can attract

Mate-retention strategies   According to the evolutionary approach, these are strategies driven by sexual jealousy that are used by one partner to deter their mates from infidelity and/or desertion; such strategies include threats, violence and emotional manipulation

Meta-analysis   A method of combining a number of studies on the same theme in order to detect trends in the behaviour being studied

Negative reinforcement   The situation where the occurrence of a behaviour is increased by removing an unpleasant stimulus, e.g. being in a relationship may be negatively reinforced as it removes feelings of loneliness or sadness

Operant conditioning   An explanation of learning that sees the consequences of behaviour as of vital importance to the future recurrence of that behaviour. If a behaviour is followed by a desirable consequence, it becomes more frequent; if it is followed by an undesirable consequence, it becomes less frequent

Polygynous   Being married to more than one woman at a time

Positive reinforcement   A stimulus that increases the frequency of a particular behaviour because of the pleasant rewards it brings, e.g. being in a relationship is positively reinforced as it brings rewards such as companionship, sex and intimacy

Proximate cause   The explanation of a particular trait or behaviour in terms of immediate (e.g. physiological, environmental) causes, to be contrasted with an ultimate cause

Reactive attachment disorder (RAD)   A severe disorder characterized by a child's failure to develop social abilities; RAD can be caused by a number of factors, including child neglect, abuse, abrupt separation from caregivers or frequent changes in caregivers (such as in children's homes)

Reductionist   An approach to behaviour that explains a complex set of facts, entities, phenomena or structures (e.g. the formation of relationships) by another, simpler set (e.g. the matching hypothesis, which focuses on the need for matching)

Sexual selection   The observation that individuals possess features that make them attractive to members of the opposite sex (intersexual selection), or help them to compete with members of the same sex for access to mates (intrasexual selection)

Social desirability   In the context of interpersonal attraction, those traits or characteristics that make an individual attractive or desirable as a partner, including physical attractiveness, status, wealth and popularity

Social desirability bias   In research studies, a tendency for participants to respond in a way that will be viewed favourably by others

Social exchange theory   A perspective that sees all social behaviour as being subject to the goal of maximizing benefits and minimizing costs

Ultimate cause   The explanation of a particular trait or behaviour in terms of ancestral (i.e. adaptive, functional) causes, to be contrasted with a proximate cause

Index